Succeeding in your Application to University

How to prepare the perfect UCAS statement

Second Edition

Matt Green

LEARNING MEDIA

First edition 2007
Second edition September 2011

ISBN 9781 4453 7961 6
Previous ISBN 9780 9556 7461 7

British Library Cataloguing-in-Publication Data
A catalogue record for this book is available from the British Library

Published by
BPP Learning Media Ltd
BPP House, Aldine Place
London W12 8AA

www.bpp.com/health

Typeset by Replika Press Pvt Ltd, India
Printed in the United Kingdom

Your learning materials, published by BPP Learning Media Ltd, are printed on paper sourced from sustainable, managed forests.

Contents

Contents

About the Publisher

BPP Learning Media is dedicated to supporting aspiring professionals with top quality learning material. BPP Learning Media's commitment to success is shown by our record of quality, innovation and market leadership in paper-based and e-learning materials. BPP Learning Media's study materials are written by professionally-qualified specialists who know from personal experience the importance of top quality materials for success.

About the Author

Matt Green BSc (Hons) MPhil
Matt Green has spent the last six years directly helping tens of thousands of individuals successfully apply to university. It is with this extensive experience in mind that Matt has written this book to help applicants prepare an effective UCAS Personal Statement as part of their application to university.

Acknowledgements

I would like to thank all of the prospective university students I have supported in the past six years; they have enabled the writing of this book to become a reality.

I would also like to thank my editor, Jen Morris, whose dedication has made this project possible.

Preface

At the time of writing, I have been supporting prospective university students with their university application for the past seven years and, in that time, I have amassed a wealth of experience and insight into the ingredients which go into composing an outstanding university Personal Statement. When I first began supporting individuals with their university application I found that the vast majority felt they received very little in the way of guidance – a situation which can only result in a below par Personal Statement and a significantly reduced chance of a successful application for those concerned. It was with this conviction to 'level the playing field' within the university application process that I made the decision to write this book.

According to UCAS, of the approximately 700,00 applicants to universities in the UK in 2010, around 490,000 were successful. To put it bluntly, around 70% of applicants were successful. To use an analogy, if you were in the Wild West and challenged to a game of Russian Roulette involving a pistol with one of its four bullet chambers loaded, would you consider a 70% chance of surviving good enough odds? Would you fancy your chances? It is precisely this situation which I am dedicated to addressing: removing the uncertainty from your university application.

Drawing upon my extensive experience of all aspects of applying to university, I embarked upon writing this guide in order to share my wisdom in planning, writing and improving a Personal Statement. This guide represents a comprehensive 'one-stop-shop' for all those intending to apply to a UK university via the Universities and College Admissions Service (UCAS), and who therefore must write a Personal Statement. In this guide I cover the entire university application process: from the initial decision to study at university to the final careful edit of your completed Personal Statement, along with everything in between. The advice, suggestions, recommendations and tips included in this guide apply to many degree subjects, all types of student, including school leavers, mature and overseas students, as well as parents and teachers.

Please note that the examples contained within this book are for guidance purposes only and must not be used as part of your application. BPP Learning Media does not agree with plagiarised applications and fully supports the crackdown on plagiarism mounted by UCAS, through the use of electronic systems to counter applicants merely cutting and pasting examples into their own application.

I hope that you find this guide both informative and helpful and would like to wish you the best of luck with your university application.

Chapter 1
Background

Background

The structure of this guide

In publishing this guide, our aim is to steer you through every stage of the university application process. Before we proceed to the main body of this guide, on planning and writing your Personal Statement, we will cover a broad range of other factors which are crucial to consider when writing your UCAS Personal Statement.

Indeed, these factors can be said to underpin it; such as choosing a university and course, whether to apply for more than one subject and the pros and cons of taking a gap year. In taking this approach we believe that, by the time you come to read the sections guiding you through the process of planning and writing your Personal Statement, you will have a good idea of the effect your Personal Statement should have on the admissions tutors, as well as a clearer idea of what you should include based on the decisions you have made regarding your future.

Through analysing first rate examples of Personal Statements, breaking them down into their constituent parts, discussing common 'do's and don'ts' and providing advice on style, phrasing and content, we have put together a logical, step-by-step guide to producing an engaging and compelling university Personal Statement which will make the best possible impression on admissions tutors.

The structure of this guide is simple and is divided roughly into two sections. The first section addresses the preparation for writing your Personal Statement. It includes some background to UCAS and the application process, a little about choosing the right course and the right university and then, step-by-step, we take you through everything you need to include in your Personal Statement. The second section covers the actual writing of the Personal Statement, discussing layout, vocabulary, style and proofing the final version.

Drawing on our extensive expertise in the field of university applications, we have written this guide in order to share with you the ingredients which should go into producing an attention grabbing, expertly written and highly impressive university Personal Statement. Through a series of 'before and after' examples, we will deconstruct both good and bad Personal Statements, as well as analyse the factors which influence an admissions tutor to either reject or accept an application, and discuss the structure, content and 'buzzwords' which admissions tutors look for in a successful Personal Statement.

A large part of our focus will be on 'reverse engineering' statements, that is to say picking them apart to give us a clearer idea of how the constituent parts fit and flow together to achieve the desired outcome, i.e. an offer of a place on your chosen course.

The importance of the university Personal Statement

Your university Personal Statement is hugely important, arguably **the** most important passage you will ever write about yourself. As more and more universities move away from routinely interviewing applicants, the Personal Statement section of the UCAS application represents your first and last chance to make a strong, lasting and positive impression on the admissions tutors. Bearing in mind that university is a place where many people really develop as an individual, experience new things and ultimately determine their future career, the importance of your UCAS Personal Statement should not be underestimated. However, nor should the prospect of writing it be one you should fear. Far from it – it should be viewed as your opportunity to tell the world exactly why you are a special person, and to convince your chosen universities that they would be foolish not to offer you a place to study on your chosen course.

The art of writing is in the expression of ideas or information in a controlled, well crafted but ultimately compelling fashion. The key to great writing is in the balance of content and form: a voluminous vocabulary and a poet's aptitude for eloquent expression are all well and good, but they can appear superficial in the absence

3

of an interesting subject or supporting facts. Likewise the most compelling idea or important information will lose all of its impact and interest if it is buried in reams of clumsy, tedious and poorly constructed prose. Ensuring that the content and expression work together to impress the reader is a skill in itself. So how exactly does this little essay on the essence of fine writing relate to your university Personal Statement?

Imagine the university selection process from the point of view of an admissions tutor. Picture your desk lost beneath a heap of innumerable Personal Statements: are you relishing the prospect of carefully reading through them all, pausing every now and then to marvel at the number of extra-curricular activities here, nodding in admiration at the achievement of a Gold Duke of Edinburgh Award there?

If you have detected that this question carries with it a hint of cynicism, then we are sure you appreciate the point we are trying to make: admissions tutors read hundreds of Personal Statements each year, and so it is imperative that yours makes an immediate, lasting and obviously positive impact. In short, you need to 'stand out from the crowd'. While it is true that you can do little to improve **what** you will say (short of participating in a few last minute extra-curricular activities in a desperate bid to appear super keen), it is well within your power to vastly improve **how** you will say it. In business this is termed as 'selling yourself' but, to put a slightly less commercial spin on it, it is essentially all about giving the best possible account of yourself in order to move one step closer to realising the hopes and aspirations you hold for your future.

With over six years experience of delivering bespoke help and support to prospective university students and schools, we have amassed a wealth of insider insight into the university admissions process, and have distilled a winning formula for writing engaging and, most importantly, successful Personal Statements.

Key points

Your university Personal Statement might be the first and last chance you have to impress the admissions tutors.

In the increasingly competitive arena of university applications, it is important to spend time and effort in composing and perfecting your Personal Statement.

How a UCAS Personal Statement enhances your university application

In terms of how your university application will be assessed, there are four crucially important strands:

- Your predicted grades
- Your employment history (more important for mature applicants)
- Your character reference
- Your Personal Statement

Although you have some degree of control over the person you choose to provide a reference for you, by the time you come to put together your application form, your predicted grades and reference lie largely outside of your control. The only aspect of your application over which you have complete control is your Personal Statement. Another factor to consider is that, even if you have been predicted three As at A level, if you are applying to a particularly competitive or over-subscribed course, such as Medicine or English respectively, then the vast majority of your fellow applicants will have been predicted similarly impressive grades. In this situation, it will be the Personal Statement which will be used as the chief criteria on which judgements over acceptance or rejection are based. Similarly, supposing that your reference is full of glowing praise – so will those of the vast majority of other applicants, because if anyone needs a reference, it is common sense that they will ask people who they anticipate will speak highly of them. So, having established that great predicted grades and a glowing reference are par for the course in the world of university applications, we are left with the conclusion that the most important aspect of your university application is your Personal Statement.

Ultimately, a Personal Statement represents your opportunity to introduce yourself to the admissions tutors in order to give them a clear idea of you as a person, along with what makes you 'tick'.

Key point

Remember, whilst your grades and reference are equally important, your Personal Statement is the only element of your UCAS application that is completely within your control.

Chapter 2

Applying to university through UCAS

Applying to university through UCAS

What is UCAS?

The acronym UCAS stands for 'Universities and Colleges Admissions Service'. UCAS is the organisation that has sole responsibility for co-ordinating applications made to practically all full-time undergraduate degree programmes at universities in the UK. The overwhelming majority of higher education institutions in the UK are members of UCAS.

Therefore, if you are intending to apply to study for an undergraduate degree in the UK, you will have to apply through UCAS, rather than direct to the universities themselves. Quite obviously, this rule applies to all UK residents, yet there is a diverse range of applicants to whom this rule also applies – namely European Union citizens and other international applicants.

There are two distinct ways to apply to university through UCAS:

* Through your school or college
* Independently

For more information on applying independently, visit the UCAS website (www.ucas.com). You cannot apply directly to a UK university for an undergraduate course. All applications must be made through UCAS using the somewhat daunting UCAS form (now an electronic form). UCAS are now encouraging all applicants to apply electronically via the UCAS website rather than in the old paper format. Apart from in exceptional cases, the UCAS form no longer exists in paper format, although the electronic application process still requires all of the information that would have been included in the old 'paper' format.

OK, so that's the background information dealt with, but what about the logistics of applying? Well, we've whittled all the relevant information down for you, and presented it here in a handy paragraph.

*To apply to a university you must submit **one** online application per calendar year via the UCAS website. If you are in full-time education then this process will be co-ordinated by your school or college. However, if you are applying independently then you need to register direct through the UCAS website (note: there is a small charge payable for this which will depend on the number of courses you wish to apply to). Although you only submit one application, you have the opportunity to select up to five courses, in order of preference. The beauty of the UCAS system is that these choices remain completely confidential throughout the entire application process, which basically means that the universities to which you have applied remain unaware of your other choices, or indeed where they rank in your order of preference.*

For those of you applying to study Medicine, Dentistry or Veterinary Science, you are still entitled to select five courses, but are only permitted up to four in your subject of preference, although the remaining course choice can be used to apply to a completely different course i.e.

1.   Medicine
2.   Medicine
3.   Medicine
4.   Medicine
5.   Biomedical Science

Oxbridge applicants (those applying to colleges of Oxford and Cambridge) together with Medical, Dental and Veterinary Science applicants differ in that candidates must submit their application by mid October the year before they intend to commence their studies. Also, if you do intend to apply to Oxford or Cambridge, you cannot apply to both universities in the same application, i.e. in the same year.

The scope for choosing courses in your subject area of preference gets even slimmer for individuals wishing to apply to Art and Design Route B courses, who are only permitted to choose up to three Art and Design related courses, which must be in order of preference.

There is a compensating factor however, in that the application window for Route B applicants is much wider, extending until March in order to allow you the time to compile a portfolio of work which will form part of your application.

Unless you are rejected by all of your chosen universities and have to go through the process of Clearing (see chapter on Clearing) you should receive any offers by the end of March. Offers are either conditional (dependent on upcoming exam results) or unconditional. Once you have heard back from all the universities to which you have applied, you are required to accept two choices, one Firm Acceptance and one Insurance Acceptance. The other three of your choices will, at this point, have effectively been declined. For further information on the UCAS application process, visit the UCAS website (www.ucas.com).

Key points

Everyone can make up to five course choices, but those applying to study Medicine, Dentistry or Veterinary Science can only make four choices in their chosen subject, whilst applicants to Art and Design Route B courses are only permitted to choose up to three Art and Design-related courses.

Although timescales vary between subjects, you should aim to submit your application no later than January of the same year you intend to commence studying i.e. January 2012 to enter university in September 2012. However, you can submit your application as early as September of the previous year which, in this example, would be September 2011.

Key dates: How to apply and when

Unless you intend to apply in the Welsh language (*Helo i'n holl ddarllenwyr o Gymru!*), your UCAS form must be completed and submitted online, via the UCAS website. UCAS no longer accept paper applications (although there are exceptional circumstances), so you will obviously need to use a computer with internet access in order to compile and submit your application. Below is a timeline of important dates to bear in mind when planning your university application:

Time of year	Event
Mid August	Clearing begins
Mid September	Clearing applications close
Early September	Applications made via UCAS now accepted
Mid October	1. Deadline for applications to Oxford and Cambridge 2. Deadline for applications to Dentistry, Medicine and Veterinary Medicine/Science courses
Early January	Applications for Art and Design Route B courses now accepted
Mid January	Recommended closing date for applications made from the UK or EU to receive a decision by late March, including Art and Design applications via Route A
Mid March	UCAS Extra commences
Late March	1. Deadline for applications for Art and Design Route B courses (although the earlier you apply the better, to avoid the perennial last minute rush!) 2. Applicants who applied before the mid January deadline should receive notice of any offers
Late June	Closing date for applications for entry in Autumn before Clearing commences
Mid August	1. Publication of A level results 2. Clearing begins
September	Commence your studies onwards

The above dates, although correct for this year's intake, should be used as a guide. We strongly advise that you check the UCAS website for the exact dates for the year in which you are applying. You should aim to complete the writing of your Personal Statement by early October of the year before you intend to enter university although, to receive a decision by late March, the deadline for applicants is mid January.

Bearing in mind that your Personal Statement can take anywhere between three and six weeks to perfect (from the moment you start 'thought showering' on a blank piece of paper to the final proofread) you should start the process of writing your Personal Statement in early August in the year before you intend to commence your studies.

What is on the UCAS form?

There are ten sections to the online UCAS application form, but don't be disheartened, some are much more straight-forward than others. Let's turn our focus on exactly what goes into a completed UCAS application.

1.   **Registration**
       At the risk of stating the blindingly obvious, before you can start working on your application, you need to register (if you are applying through a school or college this will be done for you). UCAS require you to enter your personal details, such as your name, address and date of birth. In addition, there is a terms and conditions section, which you should read through. If you are applying independently of a school or college, UCAS will generate a username for you, and prompt you to create your own password. Together these form your login details, which you will need every time you visit the site to work on your application.

2.   **Personal details**
       A relatively straightforward section – simply complete any details not automatically filled in with the details you entered during registration. UCAS also ask you to provide further information which universities invariably want to know about you, such as your nationality, residency status and whether you have a disability.

3.   **Additional information**
       If you are a UK resident, UCAS want to know details of any extra-curricular activities you have undertaken which are

relevant to your course choice, as well as other information, such as your nationality and ethnic origin, purely for the purpose of equal opportunities monitoring.

4. **Choices**

This is where you enter the names and codes of the courses and higher education institutions to which you are applying. Don't worry about ordering your choices, the UCAS website will arrange them in alphabetical order. For each choice, UCAS will ask you whether you intend to live at home or in student accommodation and whether you intend to defer entry and for how long.

5. **Education**

Fairly obvious this one – simply enter details of the schools or colleges you have attended, together with your qualifications (you should include all relevant qualifications, whether you have already attained them or if you are currently taking any). It is imperative that this information is entered correctly, as it is an important factor in determining whether a university will make you an offer of a place to study at their institution.

6. **Employment**

This is where you should list full details of your work experience. It may be that you have not yet had a job of any kind, in which case you must confirm that the section is complete, to let UCAS know that you have not merely missed it out!

7. **Personal Statement**

Along with your predicted / actual grades and your reference, your Personal Statement is far and away the most important part of your application. Since this is the principle subject of this guide, we won't dwell on it here.

8. **Reference**

UCAS require a reference from someone who knows you well enough to comment on your academic ability and suitability for further study. If you are currently at school or college then this will be arranged for you and will probably be your head of Sixth Form or headteacher. If you are applying independently, ideal candidates for a reference could include a former teacher, careers adviser or a professional person who knows you well. You must ensure that your referee writes their reference and returns it to you, to allow you to enter it into this section of the form (please note, if you are applying through a school or college, this stage will be co-ordinated for you).

9. **Declaration**

After reading this section carefully, you should confirm that you agree to the terms in order to progress to the payment section.

10. **Pay and send**

If you are applying through your school or sixth form college, this section will not apply. For everyone else, you are required to pay the application fee using a credit or debit card (see the UCAS website for further information on fees).

The importance of your reference

Together with your Personal Statement, it is vital that the reference you include with your application is supportive. If you are applying through your school or college, they will co-ordinate your application, including your reference. For those applying independently of an academic institution, the following information will prove useful.

Your reference needs to be written by someone who can provide an academic viewpoint on you and who knows you well. It is no good giving a character reference, such as a family friend, as this carries no weight compared to a head of year or college principal, and is unlikely to be accepted by UCAS. If you are currently at school or college, your reference will normally be given by your head of year, headteacher or college tutor. It is vital that your referee is made aware of the subject you intend to study at university and is supportive of your application. All your hard work composing a sparkling Personal Statement may be wasted if the reference you are given is vague and non-supportive.

Remember, you are well within your rights to ask to see your reference! It is important to approach a referee who you know will present you in the best possible light. If you are currently at, or have only recently left school, you should ask:

- Your headteacher or college principal
- Your personal tutor or an appropriate teacher

If you are applying independently of a school or college, you should ask someone who knows you well enough to provide your reference but, more importantly, someone who knows you in a professional context.

Likely candidates could include:

- Your employer
- A senior colleague if you undertake voluntary work
- A further education tutor, if you have undertaken a recent, relevant course
- A former teacher or headteacher

As with your Personal Statement, your reference should be no longer than 4,000 characters, including spaces, and 47 lines of text, including blank lines between paragraphs. If you are applying independently of a school or college, you will need to copy and paste your reference into the appropriate section of the UCAS site. The procedure for submitting your reference, including formatting information, is exactly the same as for your Personal Statement. For further information regarding your reference, and step-by-step instructions, see the UCAS website.

Top tip

Remember, you are well within your rights to ask to see your reference!

Chapter 3
Where and what to study

Chapter 3

Where and what to study

Choosing a course

Some people decide on the subject they want to study at university at an early age, due to some formative experience. Whether you have wanted to be an engineer ever since your parents took you to the Ironbridge Gorge Museum aged 12, or whether you are on the verge of tossing a coin to decide between three or four subjects, it is vital that you make a clear, final decision as to what you want to study before you embark on writing your Personal Statement. Bearing in mind that you will spend at least the next three years studying your chosen course, it is advisable to devote some serious thought to it now. You should consider the following:

- What do you enjoy learning about? What 'pushes your buttons'?
- Do you have any career plans? Which courses are most relevant to these?
- What does a particular course offer?
- Would you like to do a sandwich course?
- Does the university you wish to attend offer that particular course?

It is recommended that you consult a careers advisor and actually visit the universities you are considering applying to. This will enable you to make an informed decision as to the subject you would like to study and the university you would like to attend. Also, think about whether you are more suited to a modular course as opposed to one which comprises only final exams.

This will be especially important if you have poor exam technique or tend not to work particularly well in the pressurised environment of an end of term revision binge! Whilst it is important to listen to the advice of your parents, friends, teachers and your careers advisor, the ultimate decision as to which university you wish to study at has to lie with you. It is a big future-defining decision and, as such, is not one which should be made on a whim: after all, it is a decision which will affect the next three years of your life, and in some cases more.

Useful websites:
www.ukcoursefinder.com
www.ucas.com

Key point

When choosing a course to study at university, think about whether you want to be qualified to enter a particular profession as soon as you graduate, or whether you would be prepared to undergo further, specialist training. For example, graduating in courses such as Veterinary Science will qualify you to enter a specific profession, whereas courses such as English, Music, Geography or Mathematics will not (although they are all highly regarded in a broad range of employment sectors).

Choosing a university

The crossroads: Why university?

In recent years the UK has witnessed a rising tide of university applications and admissions. With university admissions at a high water mark, you would be forgiven for thinking that an undergraduate degree has been devalued, but graduates from UK universities earn, on average, £160,000 more over the course of their working lives than those who enter the world of work after their A levels. Granted, stories about 19-year-old plumbers and electricians earning upwards of £70k a year are ubiquitous and, while it is undoubtedly true that skilled tradesman are at something of a premium these days, a degree has the power to open many more doors, not to mention the opportunities undergraduate life affords in terms of forging life-long friendships and providing you with an invaluable and transferable set of life experiences and skills. Undergraduate life is a stimulating mix of academic rigour, rampant socialising and character-forming encounters with people from all backgrounds and walks of life. From the lecture hall abounding with fascinating ideas and the crammed tutorial room buzzing with the stimulating cut-and-thrust of debate, to the halls of residence thumping with music and pervaded by the aroma of vodka and real ale, university is a truly defining experience in anyone's life. Future friendships, careers and even life partners are all to be found during the course of life as an undergraduate. Having said all of that, we're running ahead of ourselves a little. At the moment, university is an ambition, an aspiration that you need to realise. If you are totally sure that university is the path for you, then you must focus all your efforts and energies into securing a place at one of your top choice universities.

Decisions, decisions

For some people, choosing a university is a *fait accompli*, usually as a result of their desire to stay in their home town. For everyone else, choosing which universities to apply to invariably involves a constellation of considerations which must be contemplated and assigned a relative weighting. For instance, it may be that you are particularly attracted to the course content or a particular lecturer, whose area of expertise means that the department offers modules in areas of your subject which you have a particular interest in pursuing. It may be that the department of your first choice university is particularly renowned as an international centre for a particular branch of your subject. Alternatively, it may be that you are hankering for the bright lights and cosmopolitan bustle of a big city, having spent your childhood in a rural area where the most fun to be had revolved around a bus shelter and a litre of cider.

Other, arguably more secondary considerations, include the opportunity to join a specific club or society, and the lure of excellent facilities, such as the university library (as in the case of the John Rylands library at the University of Manchester) or the links a department has with industry, and the resultant opportunities for practical work experience (as in the case of the Biosciences Department at Kent University, which enjoys good links with the pharmaceutical company Pfizer).

At the time of writing this guide, the UK has over 300 universities and colleges of higher education. For anyone without a firm idea of **where** and **what** they intend to study, choosing a university might seem like an arbitrary 'pin in the map' exercise. However, there are a number of resources, of varying help and use, available to inform and guide your decision. The obvious place to start researching is by getting hold of university prospectuses, although the information within these can be somewhat vague and limited, so it is also advisable to visit university websites.

A big factor in your final decision will be whether you want to move away from your home town. Particularly if you have never lived away from home before, or if you tend to have trouble adapting to new situations, it is hugely important that you visit anywhere you are considering applying to, in order to get a feel for the place. For example, is it a bustling, cosmopolitan city, or a sedate, rural town? Also, bear in mind any specific issues relating to you, such as dyslexia, and find out what the universities offer by way of facilities to suit your particular needs. You may find that the quickest and most effective route to solving your university conundrum is to talk the situation through with someone else. Your first port of call should be the careers adviser at your school or college, but equally good people to chat to are Personal Tutors, university admissions staff, existing university or college students and people who currently work in the field you wish to enter.

Not having a clear idea of where you want to study really needn't represent a cause for concern. The key here is to draw up a short list and actually visit any of the universities on your list which you remain uncertain about. A useful resource to help you hone in on the university most suited to you comes in the form of a website, www.opendays.com. This is a definitive source of information on open days for universities in the UK. You can either search by month or search their exhaustive database of institutions. As well as being a completely free resource, the site also allows you to book your place at certain open days, as well as find out travel information. Alternatively, you can:

- Read the university prospectus online
- Read the course information at www.ucas.com

Open days provide the perfect opportunity for you to really scope out a university, and get a sense of the facilities on offer, as well as a general 'feel' for the place and the surrounding location. After all, you wouldn't buy a car without first going for a test drive, let alone without even seeing it – a good analogy bearing in mind that students can graduate with debts (excluding tuition fees) of around £25,000 (although a prudent approach can bring this figure down to around the £10,000 mark!). Open days usually take the form of a guided tour around the campus and, in some cases, you might get the chance to attend talks on subject-specific issues, as well as meet staff from your prospective department. Remember, you need to concentrate on the facilities that matter to you, which might include the teaching facilities in your department, the university library or even prices in the student union bar!

The following are a couple of important considerations which you should bear in mind when deciding which universities you would like to study at:

- Smaller campus-based universities tend to have more of a community feel, and generally score highly in terms of student satisfaction.
- You should be realistic. If you have been predicted BCD at A level then you should think very seriously about shelving your ambition to study at an Oxbridge college. By working out your UCAS tariff you can match your score with the entry requirements for your chosen course at different universities. For more detailed information, the UCAS website contains standard offers for all courses.

Top tip

Don't be put off by universities which are relatively low in the rankings. Many lower ranked institutions are actually very highly ranked for certain subjects. For example, Strathclyde University is ranked overall 41st by *The Good University Guide*, but its Pharmacology and Pharmacy department is ranked in the top ten for that subject in the UK. There are countless other examples of lower ranked universities which are ranked very highly in one or two specific areas.

Applying to different subjects

If you have enjoyed studying all of your A level subjects equally, you may not feel in a position to choose just one subject to pursue at degree level when it comes to completing your UCAS application a year before you will actually commence your university studies. Although there is nothing to stop you applying to university to study more than one course, this can pose problems when trying to write your Personal Statement.

Due to the inherent drawback of only being able to submit one Personal Statement, if you are applying to study more than one subject then you will inevitably find it difficult to tailor your Personal Statement to be relevant to different subjects. For example, you might have a burning ambition to study Law, but feel that you are more likely to be offered a place to study Accountancy given your academic record. In this scenario, if you are absolutely convinced that you want to keep your options open then it is far easier to write a general Personal Statement which covers both Maths and Accountancy, as they both involve working with numbers, than it is to write one to cover both Accountancy and Law, each of which require an entirely separate set of skills.

 Useful websites:
www.opendays.com
www.push.co.uk
www.ucas.com
http://extras.thetimes.co.uk/public/good-university-guide-landing (there is a subscription fee for this site)
www.guardian.co.uk/education/universityguide

Before deciding to apply to multiple courses, you need to weigh up the pros and cons – by not targeting your Personal Statement to a particular subject are you weakening your application? However, many people do apply to study unrelated courses as part of their five choices and are successful in gaining offers of places to study, so you shouldn't necessarily feel inhibited from doing so.

Top tip

If you are struggling to decide between several subjects, you might wish to consider a combined degree course, such as English Literature and Theatre Arts, History and Classics or Business and International Politics. There are many combinations of subjects available, so consult the prospectuses of the institutions you are considering applying to in order to find out more.

Grade requirements and competition for courses

Taking a general, holistic view, the competition for university places is becoming increasingly hard fought with each passing year. This is largely due to the increasing numbers of applicants to universities in the UK and is expected to continue increasing each year. And yet the situation isn't quite as straightforward as all this suggests.

It goes without saying (but we're going to say it anyway) that competition for places differs drastically between courses. In the case of Medicine and Dentistry, just under 41% of applicants were successful in 2005, whereas for Mass Communications-related courses, the acceptance level was a much healthier 95%. To give you a rough indication of how competition for places and success rates differ between subjects, the following (approximate) percentages represent the number of applicants accepted to study their chosen subject in a given year:

Subject area	% of applicants accepted
Creative Arts and Design	76%
Social Studies	82%
Law	86%
Historical and Philosophical Studies	90%
Biological Sciences	92%
Linguistics and Classics	92%

European Languages and Literature	94%
Engineering	96%
Architecture	96%
Maths and Computer Science	97%
Physical Sciences	105%
Science combined with Social Sciences or Arts	183%

To reiterate, the higher the percentage, the higher the number of applicants who were accepted. The more mathematically inclined amongst you will have noticed the seemingly impossible figures for Physical Sciences and Sciences combined with Social Sciences or Arts. The reason for this is that the number accepted to study courses which fall into these brackets exceeded the number who applied. Whilst we concede that listing these as greater than 100% is somewhat of a mathematical *faux pas*, these seemingly impossible statistics can be explained in one word: Clearing. For example, whilst 10,000 people might apply for a particular course, there may be 15,000 places available in universities across the UK, and so the 5,000 shortfall in applications is made up during the Clearing process. Should you find yourself in the position of having to go through Clearing, think long and hard about applying to subjects which are traditionally undersubscribed. For further information on the Clearing process see Chapter 5.

Chapter 4

Important factors to consider

Important factors to consider

Tuition fees and financial help

Ever since the scrapping of student grants, prospective undergraduates have had to factor the looming spectre of tuition fees into their deliberations over where to study. As tuition fees continue to creep upwards, the idea of staying at home and studying at the nearest university to your home town might seem like a tempting one. The principle cost of undergraduate study comes in the form of tuition fees, which since the increase of these in 2011 vary any where between £5,000 and £9,000 per year. Your student loan will cover these, and for more information on student loans visit the Student Loans Company website (www.slc.co.uk). On top of your tuition fees, you will have to factor in the cost of living away from home. This can be broken down as follows:

- Accommodation
- Books and related study materials
- Clothes
- Food
- Household bills (gas, electricity, water, contents insurance etc.)
- Leisure and sport
- Socialising
- Travel

There are a number of sources of additional financial support available to undergraduate students, and these include:

- Access to learning funds
- Adult dependants' grant
- Benefits
- Bursaries and scholarships
- Childcare grant
- Disabled students' allowances
- Educational grants and charitable trusts
- Higher education grant
- Maintenance grant
- Parents' learning allowance
- Part-time work

- Special support grant
- Tuition fee grant

For further information on eligibility criteria, and how to apply for any of the various bursaries, grants and benefits available, see the following list of useful websites.

Useful websites:
www.slc.co.uk
www.scholarship-search.org.uk
www.direct.gov.uk/en/EducationAndLearning/University
AndHigherEducation/index.htm

Top tip
To work out your own personal budget go to
www.direct.gov.uk/yourfuture

Taking a gap year: Help or hindrance?

Gap years are becoming an increasingly popular hiatus between school and higher education. According to the Year Out Group (a trade association for gap year companies) of the 200,000 British people who take time out each year, 40,000 are school leavers who have secured a place at university but chose to defer entry for a year. A further 40,000 of this 200,000 figure are waiting for their A level results before applying, while another 50,000 of those who take a gap year leave school without any firm plans, or a clear sense of direction for their future.

Gap year placements fall into four categories:

- Short language or specialist courses and cultural exchanges (expeditions, conservation, trekking and personal development programmes) led by groups such as Raleigh International, Quest Overseas and Trekforce Expeditions.
- Specialist science projects for Non-Governmental Organisations (NGOs), with whom students choose a placement

related to their area of study and work as a research assistant.

- Voluntary work placements of up to 12 months (Project Trust, Teaching and Projects Abroad and i-to-i offer these types of projects).
- Full-time structured work placements in companies directly related to the student's area of prospective study (as offered by The Year in Industry, among others).

Pros

The decision to undertake a gap year represents a long term investment which you can 'cash in' when it comes to securing your first job upon graduating. With such intense competition for jobs among graduates, having details of a gap year on your CV will put you in a very strong position when it comes to applying for jobs. As well as demonstrating your maturity in adapting to new situations and living away from home, the fact that you undertook conservation, humanitarian or other types of project work could potentially impress a future employer.

Cons

There is a case to be made that, whilst a great many gap year students have a generally positive experience, it is not unheard of for young people to arrive at a project only to find that there is little direction, structure and support available. Also, bear in mind that you could be expected to pay many thousands of pounds to teach English as a foreign language, undertake humanitarian work or join a conservation project, which must beg the question 'does such a gap year represent value for money?'

 Useful websites:

www.yearoutgroup.org
www.gapyeardirectory.co.uk
www.realgap.co.uk
www.i-to-i.com
www.raleighinternational.org
www.projects-abroad.co.uk
www.vso.org.uk
www.wwv.org.uk

Key point

Research your options thoroughly before taking a gap year, to ensure that you make the most of what should be a very enjoyable and rewarding experience.

Working in industry: Sandwich course

If you are at all concerned that your degree will not be sufficient to put you 'ahead of the pack' when the time comes to find a job after graduating, but you have decided that taking a gap year is not the right choice for you, then you might wish to consider a sandwich course. Sandwich courses allow you to undertake work in an industry placement relevant to your chosen area of study.

Sandwich courses are so called because the filling of an industrial work placement is 'sandwiched' between the bread of a university course. Typically, sandwich courses are arranged in one of two ways:

- For the first three years, an alternating pattern of six months at university followed by six months in a training situation. The fourth, and final, year is spent exclusively studying at university.
- A 12 month industry placement, usually 'sandwiched' between the second and final year of an undergraduate degree. Whether you are studying Engineering, Computing, Business or a science-based degree, a sandwich course gives you the opportunity to pause your degree course and work within the industry you are intending to enter after graduating. Not only will you be paid a competitive rate for this work, but it will be directly relevant to both your degree and your intended career.

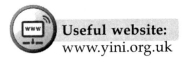

Useful website:
www.yini.org.uk

Repeating exams: Not the end of the world

With a sparkling reference and a compelling Personal Statement, you might think that falling short of your predicted grades would sound the death knell for your university application, but this simply is not the case. If lower than expected grades have led to you being rejected from your first choice course, you might want to consider retaking your A level exams, which can be done in November or January, depending on the subject and syllabus you're following. Alternatively, you might want to consider taking a year out to repeat your exams. In this scenario, you should carefully consider the merits of changing to a subject or subjects in which you stand a better chance of achieving top grades, for example switching from Maths to Economics if you are more interested in the appliance of mathematics in 'real world' scenarios as opposed to theory.

Although it might seem like the end of the world as you know it if you have to defer entry to university for a year, think of it as an opportunity to undertake activities which will enhance your Personal Statement when you re-apply next year. For instance, you could undertake voluntary work or work experience in an area directly relevant to the course you intend to study at university. 'Bouncing back' from a major setback, so to speak, demonstrates great maturity and character and will actually strengthen your chances of success next time around.

Chapter 5
The Clearing process

The Clearing process

The Clearing process is often misunderstood and stigmatised as a sign of failure, but this could not be further from the truth. Clearing is simply another path to university, and students who apply through Clearing will have the same university experience as those who secured their place through a regular UCAS application.

The vast majority of students who apply to university through Clearing do so because they didn't meet the grade requirements for the university they were applying to, but Clearing also caters for late applicants and those students who were perhaps unsure about going to university but decide to do so later on in the year. All of these applications are processed by UCAS through Clearing, which may seem complicated at first, but the process is a lot less difficult and stressful than it first appears.

According to UCAS, in 2010 approximately 690,000 students applied for a university course through UCAS, and official figures show that of the just under 480,000 accepted places throughout the UK, just under 47,000 students secured their place through Clearing. The number of applications made through Clearing deceased marginally since it began in 2004. The role of Clearing in university applications is becoming ever more important, allowing tens of thousands of students to experience university life who would otherwise have missed out.

Where first?

When you receive your results, the first step is to telephone your first choice universities. It may be that even though you haven't achieved the required grades, the university may accept you based on other factors, such as your interview or Personal Statement. If you've called your firm choice university and they don't confirm your place, the next step is to call the insurance university you have applied to as they may still have places available.

One of the most important things to remember at this point is to be open-minded. Think carefully about **why** you didn't get the grades you were expecting; are you completely sure that you wanted to get into that particular course or that particular university? If you are certain, could it be worth re-sitting an A level or two to make sure that you have the grades you need to reapply next year? If you accept that you can't get onto that course and you want to start your course immediately, then the next step is Clearing.

Clearing, UCAS and the application procedure

If you're applying through Clearing because a university didn't offer you a place, you will become eligible for Clearing as soon as UCAS acknowledge that you aren't holding any firm offers. If you are applying as a late applicant, you will be placed automatically into Clearing. Your eligibility also assumes that you have paid the full application fee; if you have only paid the reduced fee, you must pay the additional balance in order to change your status and become eligible.

How Clearing works

The Clearing process is much simpler than it first appears, but the key thing to remember is that applying through Clearing will require a lot of input from you in order to get the most out of it, i.e. a place at a good university to study your desired course. The more effort you make to choose courses, visit universities and call admissions tutors, the more chance you will have of being offered a place. The Clearing process is only what you make of it, and you should work hard and stay positive in order to secure a place at university.

What information do I need to apply?

One of the most important documents you will need is the Clearing Passport, which is automatically sent out to you by UCAS as and when your Clearing status is confirmed. For more information on the Clearing Passport, visit the UCAS website.

Finding a course through Clearing

The first step is to find the course that you want to apply for. Immediately after the A level results are released, the UCAS website will display a complete list of course vacancies throughout the UK. The list is live and interactive, and allows you to search through the complete directory of available courses and universities.

UCAS also supply official vacancy information to the *Independent* and the *Independent on Sunday*, and from results day onwards, UCAS operate extended telephone hours, so there's always a friendly and experienced operator available to help you if you'd rather deal with a human voice (this telephone number can be found on the UCAS website).

Contacting the universities

When you have your list of courses, it's time to get on the phone and start calling the universities. This is your chance to ask anything you need to know about the course and the university, so prepare some questions and learn all you can before you make a decision. Be sure to ask about course requirements and availability; some courses will be more popular than others and might fill up more quickly. Don't forget, however, that this is also a chance for them to learn about **you**. It might be tempting to get your parents to call the universities for you, or to get some friends to help so that you can call a few at a time, but it doesn't set the best impression for the admissions tutors at the other end.

Key points

Be prepared. Make sure you have all the necessary documents, numbers and details available when you call universities.

Be available. If you can, be around on the day and be near to a phone so you can get into the Clearing process as soon as possible and have a look at courses before they fill up.

Take your time. Don't rush into anything without thinking it through properly.

Talk to someone. If you have any doubts about choosing a course, talk to your college careers adviser or a tutor who knows you well.

Chapter 6

Personal Statement overview

Personal Statement overview

The UCAS Personal Statement

The UCAS Personal Statement is your opportunity to stamp your unique mark on your university application. The Personal Statement is used by admissions tutors to select candidates for interview or to make a conditional or firm offer to an applicant. As more universities are moving away from routinely interviewing applicants, the UCAS Personal Statement is becoming increasingly important. It is also important to note that when a candidate fails to achieve their target grades, the first thing an admissions tutor will look at when deciding whether to accept the applicant following poor examination performance is their Personal Statement.

The Personal Statement section of the UCAS application form represents your chance to distinguish yourself from the thousands of other students applying to your course. It is important to structure your statement logically, using appropriate paragraphs. A sure fire way of consigning your application to the 'special filing cabinet' under the desk is to write a 'splurge' of loosely connected sentences with no real structure.

Remember, the main aims of a Personal Statement are to demonstrate:

- Your enthusiasm for your chosen area of study
- Your subject knowledge, and evidence of wider interests (through reading and relevant work experience)
- Your self-motivation and drive
- Your academic ability
- Your personality, interests, aspirations and goals
- Evidence that you are 'well-rounded' and mature, and balance school life with extra-curricular activities

Key point

A Personal Statement is used by admissions tutors to separate out candidates who appear equally strong on paper (i.e. their exam results and predicted grades). Use your Personal Statement as a vehicle for imprinting your own unique character on your application.

Gathering ideas

Once you have decided on the subject you would like to study at university, the first step you need to take when preparing to write your Personal Statement is to summarise the important points about you. Without this information you will find it very difficult to begin composing your Personal Statement. Try taking a blank piece of paper and brainstorming each point listed below. Try to write down as much as you can – at this stage it is about getting your ideas down on paper so that you have the information you need to begin composing your Personal Statement.

What type of person are you?

Committed?	Outgoing?	Productive?
Articulate?	Hardworking?	Enthusiatic?
Efficient?	Ambitious?	Motivated?
Reliable?	Self-sufficient?	Keen?
Inquisitive?	Tenacious?	Logical?
Communicative?	Independent?	Creative?
Thorough?	Diligent?	Sociable?

Why do you want to study at university?

These reasons may include:

- To be able to secure a good job when you graduate
- To follow a career that you would otherwise be unable to follow
- To enjoy the experience of meeting new people
- To explore your subject in more detail

- To explore the different activities university has to offer e.g. societies, clubs, sports etc

What has influenced your decision to study your chosen subject at university?

- Why do you want to study your chosen subject?
- What enthuses you about your subject?
- What has influenced your choice of subject: school lessons, work experience?
- What aspects/areas do you find interesting?
- How will university develop your interest in your chosen subject?

What are your academic achievements?

- What are your greatest academic achievements?
- What awards have you been recognised for?
- How do these relate to your choice of course?

What are your future goals?

- Where do you see yourself after graduating from university?
- What career path would you like to follow?
- How will attending university help you to achieve this?

What work experience do you have and how has this developed you as a person?

- What work experience do you have that is directly relevant to your application?
- How has this allowed you to experience what is involved with following a career in your subject?
- What new insights have you gained?
- How has your part-time employment developed you as a person: think in terms of interpersonal skills, managing people, time-management, adhering to deadlines etc.
- What personal skills has your work experience provided you with?

What are your extra-curricular achievements and hobbies?

- What sports do you play?
- What are your hobbies?
- How have these developed you as a person?
- Do you intend to continue these interests at university?

Key points

Think 'interview': It's worth mentioning at this early stage that, should you be called for interview, your Personal Statement will form the basis of the interviewing tutor's questions. With this in mind, you should only write about things which you would be comfortable expanding on at interview. Remember:

Don't embellish the truth or lie about anything. You will be found out at interview if you do.

Only include areas of your subject which you have a *genuine* and *informed* interest in. For example, it's no use mentioning Foucault's 'Archaeological approach to the analysis of history' or your 'Interest in the future application of quantum mechanics, for example the development of quantum computers' if you have only mentioned them to impress and would be tongue-tied if asked to discuss them at interview. *Be honest at all times.*

What a UCAS Personal Statement should contain

A well-structured, engaging and convincing university Personal Statement cannot be written in a few hours. A great deal of time and thought should go into composing one. Simply rushing will result in your application being unsuccessful. The Personal Statement is your opportunity to stand out from other applicants who possess the same academic grades. Your Personal Statement must follow a balanced but original approach – remember that admissions tutors will read through hundreds of applications, therefore you need to make your Personal Statement stand out from the crowd. You should approach writing your Personal Statement by noting down on paper information about you that will form the basis of your Personal Statement.

Your Personal Statement should address the following points:

- What subject would you like to study and why?
- What do you find interesting, what would you like to learn about in more detail? Have you prepared yourself by reading around your subject?
- What has influenced your choice of subject? – school subjects, experiences in life, work experience, career aims?
- What are you looking forward to learning about at university? (many people miss this important point out).
- Are you disciplined, motivated, hardworking? You need to demonstrate that you will be able to cope with the responsibility and pressures of studying at university.
- Your achievements in life, both academic and extra-curricular.
- How any work experience you have undertaken has improved you as a person and relates to your subject choice – transferable skills?
- How will you benefit from attending university? How will attending university develop you as an individual? Will obtaining a degree allow you to progress your intended career? Do you intend to make use of the sports, clubs and societies on offer at university?
- Showing that you intend to strike a balance between studying and trying new experiences is important!
- Who you are as a person. What makes you the person you are? What are your interests and hobbies? Are you a person with a balanced range of interests? Do you intend to pursue these at university?

A Personal Statement is exactly that – 'personal' – and must be original to attract the attention of the admissions tutors. A clear and well-planned Personal Statement gives you the best possible chance of securing an offer from your first choice university. Universities are looking for self-motivated, mature and enthusiastic individuals who will be committed to their studies whilst contributing to university life as a whole.

You should start writing your university Personal Statement as soon as possible. The more time you give yourself to prepare and write it, the better your chances will be of securing a place at one of your top choice universities.

In addition to the areas your Personal Statement must touch upon, as listed, it is also advisable to include as much of the following as is relevant to you:

- Involvement in widening participation activities (i.e. mentoring or summer schools).
- Whether you have taken steps to prepare for higher education, for example through the ASDAN Aimhigher Certificate of Personal Effectiveness.
- Participation in other programmes and activities, such as the Duke of Edinburgh Award scheme and the Millennium Volunteers and Young Enterprise schemes.

In essence, a Personal Statement is a vehicle for you to demonstrate your academic ability, dedication, maturity and ambition. However, it is imperative that you use facts to corroborate what you say, since it is easy (and all too common) for students to declare their 'hard working, conscientious and ambitious' character without introducing specific examples to support such claims. Whatever you decide to include in your Personal Statement, you must bear in mind that the admissions tutors will be looking to tick the following boxes:

- You are hard working, enthusiastic and likely to 'stick the course'.
- You are suited to the course that you are applying to study.
- You are mature, well-rounded and can handle pressure and adapt to new situations and environments.
- You have demonstrated commitment and extra-curricular interest in your chosen subject.

Top tip

Before you do anything, make sure to scour the websites and prospectuses of the universities you are applying to for any guidance or suggestions for writing your Personal Statement. Thinking about this logically, the likelihood is that the admissions tutors themselves will have provided this information, thus giving you a valuable insight into how to tailor your statement to meet their expectations.

The rules your UCAS Personal Statement needs to adhere to

Your Personal Statement must not exceed 4,000 characters, including spaces, or 47 lines of text, including blank lines between paragraphs. If you elect to use a word-processing programme to write your Personal Statement, it is likely that it will feature a word count facility, but it is advisable to use the word count feature on the UCAS website, which will tell you exactly how many characters and lines you either have to spare, or need to cut. To access this facility, simply navigate to the UCAS website, select 'Apply', sign in (or register for the first time), click on 'Statement' and you will be able to import your statement into the box on screen. By clicking 'Preview' you will be able to see, at a glance, whether your Personal Statement is under or over the character limit, and by how much.

When composing your Personal Statement, bear in mind that UCAS do not allow for fancy formatting, so any time you spend titivating your statement with **bold**, *italic* or underlined text will be wasted. This also applies to foreign characters, so if you want to cite your part-time job in a café as being instrumental in helping you to develop strong interpersonal and collaborative working skills, you will have to resign yourself to losing the accent on the 'e'. Of course, you won't be penalised if you do use any of the formatting mentioned above, and in fact many word-processing programmes automatically add foreign characters, but bear in mind that your final statement will omit any formatting, so it is advisable not to include any in the first place.

As noted earlier, in the vast majority of cases, UCAS no longer accept paper applications. One important factor to consider when submitting your application online is that the 'Apply' screen of the UCAS website will time-out after approximately 30 minutes of inactivity. Picture the scene: you're writing your Personal Statement straight into the relevant section on the UCAS website, when you get distracted by a phone call. 40 minutes pass by and because you neglected to save your progress, the website has timed out and you have lost hours of work. Although this might turn out to be a grimly familiar scenario once you are at university and writing essays, you can guard against this happening by making a point of saving your statement regularly.

Better still (and we strongly recommend this option), write your Personal Statement offline using a word processing programme and subsequently copy and paste it into the 'Apply' section to check the character and line limit.

Other formatting points to remember include:

- Write your Personal Statement in the Times New Roman font, and no smaller than point 12. This is crucial as your statement will be reduced from A4 to A5 size, i.e. reduced by half, so writing in a font size smaller than 12 could make your statement unreadable.
- Tabs will be reduced to a single space, so your submitted Personal Statement will not feature any indented lines. Single spaces at the beginning of lines will also be removed.
- Along with upper and lower case letters, and standard punctuation marks (full stops, commas, inverted commas, speech marks, colons and semi-colons) you can use any of the following symbols:

  ! £ $ % ^ & * ( ) _ + | / @ ~ [ ] ? * - =

- Common symbols which are not allowed include: € – and the special quote characters " ' ' " so remember to only use short dashes - and quotes with " and '.

It is advisable to disable the 'auto format' feature if you are writing your Personal Statement using Microsoft Word, as not doing so may mean that dashes and quotations and marks are removed from your submitted Personal Statement, which could give the impression that your grammar is poor, or that you have not proofread your statement before submitting it.

Key points

Your Personal Statement must not exceed 47 lines and/or 4,000 characters.

Use the font Times New Roman, size 12.

Type it using a word-processing programme, and subsequently paste it into the relevant section of the UCAS site.

Structuring your Personal Statement

If you were to set out on a long journey, you would naturally take with you a route map to guard against the very real possibility of getting hopelessly lost and confused. This principle applies equally to the planning and writing of your Personal Statement. You need to have a clear structure in place before you start; if you like, the skeleton to which you will add the flesh. No matter how well you write your statement, if it isn't well structured, with a logical progression of coherent and related sentences, the admissions tutors will spare themselves the headache of reading much beyond the second paragraph by consigning it to that 'special filing cabinet' we mentioned earlier! As far as possible, your statement should include:

- An introductory paragraph introducing why you would like to study your chosen subject and why you would be suitable to study at university.
- What steps you have taken to pursue your interest in your chosen subject outside of school.
- What topics you are looking forward to learning about in more detail at university.

- Specific examples of your academic/extra-curricular experiences and how these have influenced your choice of subject.
- What responsibilities you have had in and out of school and how these relate to your application.
- Details of any work experience you have (both general and specific to your subject) and how it has helped developed you as a person.
- What your future career goals are.
- A concluding sentence or two summarising your application.

So, the basic structure of your Personal Statement could look something like this:

Opening paragraph

Open with a punchy, original and attention-grabbing sentence that leads into your reasons and motivations for wishing to study your chosen course.

Main body

Reflect on your academic experiences and relate what you have enjoyed about your other A or AS level subjects to your chosen course (ensure that what you write is directly relevant to your chosen course though).

Introduce activities and achievements, both in and out of school, which demonstrate your genuine and passionate interest in your chosen course (i.e. wider reading, voluntary work experience, attendance at relevant conferences etc.). Mention any relevant work experience and reflect on the skills you have gained, along with any fresh insights into your chosen subject and how it relates to possible careers.

Write about your interests and hobbies, with emphasis on how they have developed you as a person, as well as any skills you have developed which are relevant to your intended course of study.

Conclusion

This should be a relatively short paragraph to give your Personal Statement an air of finality. You should sum up by stating exactly how and why you are suitable, in terms of both your academic ability and as a well-rounded, mature person who will contribute to university life.

Although we have suggested a 'skeleton outline' as to how to formulate and construct your Personal Statement, it is important to realise that there is no right or wrong way of writing your Personal Statement. The key is to ensure that it engages the admission tutors and that it contains all of the key points we discuss in detail throughout this chapter.

Key points

Remember, your decisions as to what to include in your Personal Statement should be guided by the following:

- Be specific, as sweeping generalities will cause your Personal Statement to 'ring hollow'.
- Be honest, if you are called to interview any 'economy with the truth' will be discovered.
- Be enthusiastic and create the impression that your intellectual 'journey' within your chosen subject has only just begun.
- Reflect on how your experiences, both in and out of school, have prepared you for the academic rigours and social opportunities of higher education.

The introductory paragraph

Please note: The following examples are intended for the purposes of guidance only and should not be used, in any way, as part of your application. Doing so could mean that your university application is rejected, as UCAS have electronic systems in place to detect instances of plagiarism.

Your first paragraph should address why you have chosen the course you intend to study. Naturally, it should also be bursting with your enthusiasm for the subject, as it must encourage the admissions tutors to read on. On one level, the first paragraph is all about the art of rhetoric: you are attempting to convince someone of your argument, which is that you are perfectly suited to the study of your chosen course.

Your opening sentence will set the tone for the rest of your Personal Statement, so it needs to be hard hitting, attention grabbing and original. As a rule of thumb, it's advisable to steer clear of the 'Ever since childhood I have been fascinated by...' school of opening lines.

Instead, think about plunging straight into an area of your chosen subject. Here is an example for International Politics:

> *'As communication technologies, the threat of international terrorism and global environmental issues continue to cause the 'global village' to become more intimately linked, there has never been a more fascinating period of history in which to study International Politics.'*

The aim of the introductory sentence of your Personal Statement is to catch the attention of the reader; namely the admissions tutor. Your introductory sentence should avoid using common introductions such as:

> *'It has always been my aim to go to university and study Linguistics...'*

> *'I would like to study Business Administration because...'*

> *'Ever since I was small I have wanted to become a Vet...'*

Every year, thousands of applicants begin their Personal Statement with similarly vague, non-specific opening lines. Instead, try to compose an introductory statement that sets the scene, grabs the attention of the reader and makes your Personal Statement stand out from the crowd. We suggest several approaches that, in our experience, succeed in making an immediate and positive impression on admissions tutors:

- Talk about an area of your chosen subject which particularly excites you:

  > *'The completion of the Human Genome Project, together with the rapid advances made in the field of Biotechnology, is something which excites me greatly. Having spent my summer holidays working at GlaxoSmithKline, I was provided with an insight into what is expected of a Research Technician and am keen to follow a career in the field of Biological Research.'*

- Open with an anecdote (although this **must** be both true and specific):

  > *'It has been my goal to apply to Business and Finance since completing my Year 10 work experience placement at my uncle's firm. The use of applied Mathematics and IT appeals to me and I am confident that the skills in quantitative analysis and critical evaluation I will gain will be extremely useful for any number of possible future career paths.'*

- Give the impression that your course choice is the result of a long and careful process of thought (this is particularly advisable in the case of a mature student):

  > *'Finding my current career unfulfilling, it has been my aim for several years to pursue a career within a healthcare environment. I have always had an interest in the workings of the human body, and thorough research into the different options available within the NHS has led me to apply to study Radiography, as I am keen to specialise in an area requiring technical knowledge as well as general nursing skills'.*

With an attention-grabbing, original opening section, you now need to fully address the reasons behind your course choice.

Justifying your choice of course

This section should be positioned near the start of the Personal Statement, as it is of paramount importance to your reason for applying to university. These sentences should grab the admission tutor's attention, and should really shout about your interest in the subject. You should aim to include an explanation as to why you have chosen your degree course. Here are some reasons to consider:

Reason for your choice of degree	How you should expand on this
You enjoy the subject.	Why do you enjoy it? Be specific.
You enjoy a specific area.	Which aspects of the subject and why?
You would like to study (x) in greater depth.	Why? What do you find interesting?
Your work experience confirmed your interest.	How? In what way?
You require your degree for a particular career.	What career and why have you chosen it?
You are interested in using theory for a particular means.	What in particular and why?

Using these prompts, you should be able to write the first paragraph of your Personal Statement. The following paragraph should be used as a guide to help you compose your own introductory paragraph:

> *'Since discovering a love of reading during a lengthy hospital stay at the age of nine, I have often found pleasure in books and this passion has continued to the present day. As a result of my keen interest, I have read a wide range of genres and this has fuelled my desire to study English at a higher level. The modernist writers particularly intrigue me and I would like the opportunity to learn more about the connection between form and content. I also find gothic writing fascinating and I particularly relished Mary Shelley's 'Frankenstein.' With regards to theoretical viewpoints, I have recently been introduced to the theories of Judith Butler. Her concepts of gender and sexuality are stimulating but complex, and I would appreciate the chance to study them further in a supported environment. Studying English at university would offer me the opportunity to broaden my literary horizons, whilst expanding my ability to interpret a text.'*

The introductory statements above immediately set the scene by way of an in-depth, yet concise introduction to the reader as to why this student would like to study their chosen subject. This is then further qualified by providing additional justification for their subject choice. It is important to communicate your enthusiasm to the admissions tutors and **explain**, through specific examples, exactly how and why you have arrived at the decision to study your chosen course, rather than merely stating your suitability in vague and sweeping terms.

Your opening paragraph could reflect the following:

- Your interest and enthusiasm for your chosen subject, as well as your reasons for choosing to pursue it at university.
- Any career plans or ambitions you might have which further explain the reasoning behind your subject choice.
- Areas of your chosen course which you have enjoyed studying, as well as those which you are looking forward to studying in greater depth at university.

It is highly unlikely that you will write an opening paragraph at your first attempt which reads as well as the example above. As long as you commit your ideas to paper, you can concentrate on rephrasing and fine tuning them when the time comes to redraft.

The next step is to write about your academic and work experiences in relation to your degree and how they have developed you as a person.

Top tips

Just as with assignments and essays, you might find it easier to write the main body of your Personal Statement first, before writing your introductory paragraph.

Alternatively, you might find it useful to write your introduction and conclusion at the same time as doing so will improve the flow of your Personal Statement and lend a sense of unity and purpose to the document as a whole.

The main body

The main body of the Personal Statement must describe you as a person in relation to your application. It is important that your Personal Statement follows a logical progression and does not jump 'backwards and forwards'. The main body could include the following, if you have not covered these areas in your introductory sentences:

- Specific examples of your academic experiences and how these have influenced your choice of subject.
- What topics you are looking forward to learning about further at university.
- What responsibilities you have had in and out of school and how these relate to your application.
- Details of work experience you have (both general and specific to your subject) and how it has helped developed you as a person, as well as the effect that this has had on confirming your course choice.
- What your future career goals are.

Having succeeded in capturing the attention of the admissions tutor, you need to ensure that you hold it. The main body of your Personal Statement should demonstrate what you have done, both in and out of school, to pursue an interest in your chosen subject. Be warned that, if this section of your Personal Statement falls flat or fails to ring true, it is unlikely that the admissions tutor will read much further.

At this stage in your Personal Statement it is time to become a little more specific and hone in on exactly what you have enjoyed most about your A level subjects, as well as to reflect on how studying for them has developed you as a person, and in what ways.

Just to recap: Your introductory paragraph introduced you to the admissions tutors with a bang, grabbing their attention, for example, through an original and personal account of the reasons behind your decision to study your chosen course. The main body of your Personal Statement must convince the admissions tutors of your academic ability, evidence of a wider interest in your chosen subject and a genuine desire to learn more about it. You should also discuss the other A level subjects you are studying and the related knowledge, skills and aptitudes you have developed which will be relevant to the study of your chosen course.

Describing your academic experiences

This part of your Personal Statement should address a few of your most notable achievements in school, and should aim to provide a clear picture of someone who is academically keen, but also an active member of school life. You should also consider the skills that you have acquired through your achievements. Here's a list of a few that may be applicable:

- Good communication skills
- Self-directed study and motivation
- Good organisational skills
- The ability to work independently or in a team
- Efficiency
- Trustworthiness
- Good problem-solving skills
- Responsibility and dedication
- Sensitivity
- Self-discipline

For an idea of how this section of your Personal Statement should flow, the following example should prove useful:

> *'Participating in the school debating team allowed me to develop my powers of rhetoric and required me to construct convincing and persuasive arguments. This can only be an asset to my studies as constructing a solid argument is essential to any essay. My success in this field was recognised when I was appointed President of the Debate Team in 2008. This position of responsibility necessitated much organisation on my part; I had to arrange our meetings, put forward topics for debate and ensure that we were fully prepared for all inter-school competitions. Through this role I learnt that effective communication skills are imperative, and the confidence I gained through public speaking is invaluable and something I would actively seek to continue at university.'*

You should also consider how to mention your other A or AS level subjects in a way that is directly relevant to your chosen course.

For example, if you are intending to study English Literature at university, and one of your other A level choices was History, you could mention what you enjoyed learning about in History, making sure to relate this to your chosen course:

> *'Studying 19th century European history, specifically the radical politics of the first quarter of the century, has provided an enlightening backdrop to my understanding of the English Romantic movement in literature, specifically the work of Lord Byron.'*

Whilst it is undeniably important to reflect on the subjects you have studied at school, the admissions tutors will be particularly impressed if you can demonstrate an interest in your chosen subject that extends beyond the classroom. Evidence of a wider, continuing interest, for example through extra-curricular reading, undertaking relevant voluntary work or attending conferences, seminars or talks, will demonstrate your genuine and deep-seated interest in your chosen subject, as well as a certain maturity and an ability to undertake self-motivated study. Whatever your chosen subject, it is likely that you pursue some aspect of it outside of school. For instance:

Subject in school	Extra-curricular activity
Music	Play in a band, run a 'swing band' for lower school pupils.
English	Creative writing, member of a book club, write for the school magazine.
Computing	Designed your school's Sixth Form magazine using a desktop publishing program.
Veterinary Science	Arranged to shadow volunteers at a local animal sanctuary.

You should aim to create the impression that you are eager and enthusiastic to learn more. As with every section of your Personal Statement, be specific. You will also need to discuss the areas of your chosen subject which hold a particular fascination for you, as well as those you are looking forward to studying in greater depth at university. An example for English might be:

> *'After reading Charlotte Gilman Perkin's 'Herland' and George Orwell's '1984', I am interested in how far visions of the future, within the utopian/dystopian genre of literature, diverge along gender lines.'*

Here is another example, this time for Actuarial Science:

> *'I look forward to developing my understanding of microeconomics and of the financial and business industries. As I hope to work in the actuarial industry it will be beneficial to study investments, insurance and pensions in great detail and I intend to take the modules that will partially exempt me from the professional exams.'*

Key points

When writing about areas of your chosen subject which you are relishing exploring further at university, it is tempting to pick very complex areas, such as string theory for Physics, hermeneutics for Media or deconstructionist theories for Philosophy.

Whilst it is advisable to demonstrate your knowledge within your chosen subject, remember that anything you include in your Personal Statement can form the basis of questioning at any subsequent interview, so ensure that you are conversant with anything you choose to write about.

Writing about your work experience

Depending on your chosen subject, this section will either be crucial (for highly competitive courses such as Medicine and Law) or otherwise just plain important (as for the majority of three year courses, such as History or Chemistry, etc.). When writing about your work experience the key word is relevance. You need to consider exactly how your work experience is relevant to your choice of course, and how it has influenced and affirmed your decision. Any type of work experience can be relevant if presented in the right context, i.e.:

'Working at my local supermarket has improved my interpersonal skills and my confidence to work independently.'

At the same time, you need to be aware that the Personal Statement must flow, thus the first sentence of this paragraph must fuse your choice of degree and your work experience, making your degree choice seem perfectly logical following your work experience.

Here are two diverse examples, which display the different ways you can write about your work experience:

'Work experience at my local town planning office has been an enlightening opportunity to increase awareness of related careers and of the role of good architecture in all areas of building. Discussing plans for housing association developments, I realised that Architecture encompasses much more than just the showcase skyscrapers and luxury apartment complexes. I hope to develop my appreciation of how, for example, the design of a housing estate can be used to promote community cohesion and to dissuade anti-social behaviour. My work experience has also shown me the importance of considering the wider infrastructure of a building, such as transport systems, in ensuring effective design.'

'My work experience at Boots Contract Manufacturing gave me an invaluable insight into relevant technological fields including robotics and supply chain management. This confirmed my decision to study Engineering and Manufacturing at university and I have extended this experience by attending a number of lectures held by the Royal Engineering Society, which afforded me a detailed view into the world of engineering, including future career prospects.'

If you have not undertaken any work experience, you should include details of any activities which are relevant to your chosen course, such as a field trip you went on with school. For example, a prospective History student could write about a trip to the Imperial War Museum, and a prospective English student could discuss the inspiration they drew from a trip to Stratford-upon-Avon to see a Shakespeare play. Other subjects which commonly involve a field trip at some stage of secondary school include Geography and Biology, and the experiences they offer, particularly if they entail a stay of several days at an activity centre, are comparable to those of a week-long work experience placement:

> *'It was through a school trip to a Biology fieldwork centre that my fascination for ecosystems and habitats really developed. Through going out 'into the field' to measure and record numbers of species in various habitats, and writing up our findings in the form of essays and statistical tables, I developed a great passion for the more practical aspects of being a biologist.'*

Top tip

Whatever you choose to write about, always bear your chosen course in mind and relate your experience to the skills you will require to be successful at university:

*'I chose to arrange four weeks of work experience at a community pharmacy and then joined a large hospital trust as a pharmacy technician full time. This work required a **methodical** and accurate approach, **close attention to detail** and **good communication skills** when explaining the correct use of a particular medication to people of varying levels of understanding. Working alongside a team of medical professionals has given me a clear understanding of the roles and function of each profession, confirming for me an interest in working as a hospital pharmacist.'*

Writing about your extra-curricular activities

This is your chance to talk about what makes you tick. Choose a few current or recent activities and achievements that demonstrate your well-rounded personality and talk about them in more detail. Of course, it is not necessarily the activities in themselves which will interest the admissions tutors, but rather how your involvement in the activities you choose to mention has developed your skills and aptitudes – in short, admissions tutors are interested to learn the extent to which your life experiences to date have shaped you into a mature, well-rounded individual.

Don't make the mistake of including every achievement dating back to your 50m swimming badge, as this kind of information is irrelevant to your application and wastes valuable space. If you are successful in a particular sport then you should make the most of this in your Personal Statement, as many universities pride themselves on their strong sporting teams and developing athletes of the future. Otherwise, mention the activities you participate in outside of school, as this is a signal to the admissions tutor that you will make an active contribution to university life.

Any advanced involvement in a particular activity, for instance, competing at regional, national or even international competitions, is especially useful in this respect and will paint an impressive picture of a focused, determined and successful individual. Be warned though, if you do stretch the truth to grab the readers' attention, you are likely to be asked about these details in an interview, and the potential for embarrassment is huge.

What follows is an example of how to discuss an extra-curricular activity in a way that sheds light on you as a person, including your aptitudes, abilities and positive character traits:

> *'I am currently completing my Duke of Edinburgh Gold Award, which has required me to complete a 50 kilometre expedition in Wales. The expedition stretched my ability to work in a team, particularly under stressful situations, and I now feel confident in my ability to do so. The Duke of Edinburgh Award has also enabled me to work as a teaching assistant in a local primary school. This challenging experience has allowed me to work with small groups of children to improve their literacy skills. It is very rewarding to follow their improvement, particularly when we can make reading into an enjoyable activity rather than a chore. I am also in the school hockey team and this has afforded me the opportunity to make new friends whilst representing my school. I would hope to continue this at university.'*

This section of your Personal Statement, whilst perhaps not as crucial as those detailing your academic and work experiences, is nevertheless very important in painting a picture of you as a well-rounded and ambitious person. People who can strike a balance between, for want of a better phrase, 'work and play', stand a much greater chance of lasting the course of an undergraduate degree. With the first draft of your Personal Statement nearly complete, the final step is to compose a concluding paragraph.

Composing your concluding paragraph

A concluding paragraph is your opportunity to return to your central 'thrust' – that you are suited to the study of your chosen subject at university. The absence of a concluding paragraph will mean that your statement will hang in the air, sound unresolved and generally give the impression that you lack focus. Concluding your Personal Statement gives the impression of control, that you have made a compelling and convincing case for your ability and suitability to study your chosen course.

The key point to make in your concluding paragraph is that you are someone who will flourish both academically and socially at university. Hopefully your Personal Statement will have presented you as a well-rounded person, and now is the time to consolidate this information. The best way to do this is to choose a few areas which link your choice of degree with your wider ambitions.

Here are some examples:

> 'In finishing, I hope I have shown how much I appreciate the opportunities made available to me at university, both academically and socially. The chance to enrich my knowledge of the English canon excites me and I do not intend to waste it. By participating fully in university life I hope to reach my full potential.'

> 'As a mature applicant undergoing a career change I have thoroughly investigated my possible career paths and can bring a dedicated and committed attitude to my studies. I have a deep interest in diet and nutrition as well as in communicating this knowledge to others, and I believe I have the motivation and skills to achieve my goal.'

> 'Together with exploring and furthering my understanding of Mathematics, I fully intend to make the most of the fantastic opportunities university has to offer. By approaching my time at university in a motivated and committed manner I feel I will be

able to strike the right balance between my academic studies and extra-curricular activities.'

Key point

Do not leave any room for doubt in the minds of the admissions tutors – take the chance to reaffirm your enthusiasm and suitability for higher study through the inclusion of a short concluding paragraph.

Chapter 7
Writing tips

Writing tips

Grammar and punctuation

It's a truism of modern life that the spelling and grammar checking feature of word-processing programs is a marvellous invention, and one which saves us all from umpteen embarrassments every day. Nevertheless, because our ever vigilant little corrective friend (I'm still talking about spell checkers here) is so assiduous in picking up on errors, we tend to develop something of a spelling and grammar 'blind spot'. Unfortunately, spelling and grammar checkers are not totally reliable, particularly if your word-processing program is set to anything other than 'UK English'. With this is mind, it's imperative that you check your Personal Statement for errors yourself, paying particular attention to the following:

American spellings

Microsoft Word is a persistent culprit in this respect, particularly if the language is set to 'US English'. In particular, you need to look out for the following, which your word-processing program may not flag up as being misspelled, depending on your language settings:

- Words ending in ~ize (organize, recognize, analyze etc.)
- Words ending in ~or (color, humor, flavor, honor etc.)

Incorrect word use: Homophones

In linguistics, a homophone is a word that is pronounced the same as another word but differs in meaning. The class of homophones that we are particularly interested in here are those that are spelled differently, but sound the same:

- Aid and aide
- Altar and alter
- Aural and oral
- Effect and affect
- Too, to and two
- Weather and whether
- Your and you're

This list could quite easily stretch to a whole page, but I'm sure you get the idea. Some sets of homophones are easier to confuse in writing than others: you're far more likely to confuse *effect* and *affect* than you are to confuse, say, *we'll* and *wheel*. As with American spellings, many word-processing programs will not identify that a word has been used out of context, for instance:

> *'I couldn't sea a thing, eye had my eyes closed.'*

The program used to write this guide, Microsoft Word, failed to identify that two incorrect words were used in the above sentence. Although you are highly unlikely to make errors as glaring as those in the above example, it serves to highlight the fundamental importance of proofreading in order to wheedle out mistakes which bypass the spelling and grammar checker of your word-processing program.

Passive voice

Without wishing to delve too deeply into the science of linguistics, the passive voice pertains to a sentence where the object of the action is more important than those who perform the action. In the active voice, the **subject** of the sentence performs the action expressed by the verb:

> *'I regularly read a variety of media in order to keep abreast of current affairs.'*

In the passive voice, the subject receives the action expressed in the verb; the subject is acted upon:

> *'Regularly reading a variety of media keeps **me** abreast of current affairs.'*

Although use of the passive voice is not incorrect *per se*, its overuse can cause your prose to seem flat, impersonal and lacking in dynamism. In many spheres of academia the passive voice is preferred, such as in scientific writing, but for the purposes of your Personal Statement, you should predominantly use the active voice, using the passive voice sparingly to vary the style.

I this, I that...

Whatever you do, don't fall into the trap of assuming that, just because you are writing about yourself, you must make reference to yourself at every available opportunity. By starting every sentence with 'I...' your statement will seem repetitive and dull (think back to a time when you were bored silly by someone's monotonous tone of voice – monotony in your syntax will have exactly the same effect on the admissions tutors!). For ideas on alternatives to beginning sentences with 'I', see the section on 'buzz words and phrases'.

Structure

Previously we identified the basic structure or 'skeleton' for writing a convincing, focused and compelling Personal Statement – now it is time to turn our thoughts to adding the 'flesh'. When thinking about how to present and phrase the information you have 'thought showered' for inclusion in your Personal Statement, it is important to bear in mind that anything you choose to include must:

1.   Be relevant to your application to university and your suitability to study there, and
2.   Be phrased fluently and presented in a logical sequence.

Although the information you have amassed may all be relevant, by simply lumping it all together you will create an incoherent series of statements guaranteed to lose the interest of the admissions tutors.

Buzzwords and phrases

It is important that your Personal Statement communicates a sense of your enthusiasm. Consider using words and phrases that will help create this impression, such as:

- Fascinating/fascinated
- Passion/passionate
- Pursue/pursuing
- Devotion/devoted
- Proud/honoured/delighted
- Relishing the prospect

Your Personal Statement also needs to create the impression of you as a mature individual who has learned and developed as a result of your life experiences so far, so try to use words which will help create this impression:

- Developed
- Honed
- Strengthened
- Maintained
- Gained
- Confirmed/reaffirmed

Remember, the admissions tutors are also looking for a range of key skills which combine to produce successful university students:

- Leadership
- Time-management
- Communication
- Teamworking
- Initiative
- Dedication/determination/commitment
- Organisation
- Responsibility

Also, rather than simply listing along the lines of 'I did (x) at (y) and I improved my (z) skills', try using variations of the following linking words and phrases:

As well as
As well as greatly enjoying Economics at A level, I have undertaken work experience at...

Having
Having worked as a volunteer at a local theatre, I have gained great insight...

Besides
Besides my active participation in the school orchestra, I am also involved in teaching...

In addition to

In addition to contributing to the Sixth Form magazine, I also…

Enabled me

Captaining the school hockey team enabled me to develop my team working skills…

Opportunity to

The opportunity to work with disabled children was challenging yet rewarding…

Provided me

My work experience at a local hospital provided me with the opportunity to…

Reinforced

My work experience has reinforced my decision to study…

Confirmed

My exam successes at A level have confirmed my interest in pursuing…

Strengthened

My decision to study Geology was strengthened by a field trip to…

To illustrate the power of language to communicate several key points in a relatively short space, consider the following sentence:

> *'Working in a multidisciplinary healthcare setting has **reinforced** my **desire** to **pursue** this **challenging career.**'*

- Reinforced – suggests that the student has given prior thought to their chosen course.
- Desire – demonstrates passion and enthusiasm.
- Pursue – implies that the student is driven, focused and committed.

- Challenging – again, this suggests that the student has gained an insight into the nature of their intended career.

Reflection

Whilst it is certainly important to think long and hard about exactly what to include in your Personal Statement, it is crucial that you afford equal, if not more time to reflecting on exactly how the experiences you mention have enabled you to develop as a person, as well as the skills you have developed as a result of your school, work and extra-curricular experiences. Never lose sight of the fact that the admissions tutors are looking for your statement to provide evidence of a mature and well-rounded individual. You need to justify what you write about through reflecting on the points you raise. The following table should give you an indication of how certain activities can be used as a springboard to convincing the admissions tutors of your aptitude and suitability for higher study:

Activity	Skills/Character traits
IT proficiency	Problem solving, logical thinking
Playing a musical instrument	Creativity, teamwork, time management, dedication
Organising and co-ordinating events	Teamwork, organisation, reliability
Voluntary work	Time management, reliability, community minded
Drama club	Speaking and listening, creativity, teamwork

So, rather than merely stating: *'I spent two months working as a volunteer at a local animal rescue centre'*, you need to reflect on what you have gained from your experience, how it developed you as a person, its relevance to your chosen course (in the case of the example below, Veterinary Science) and what it demonstrates about your character:

> *'In order to gain experience of working with animals, I undertook a two-month voluntary placement at a local animal rescue centre.*

> *Through shadowing the staff I gained a **valuable insight** into the daily duties of a Veterinary nurse, as well as **improving my confidence** through handling a range of species. I also **improved my communication and teamworking skills** by accompanying staff when returning healthy animals back to the wild.'*

No matter what your chosen subject is, reflection is vital:

> *'As an assistant director for a school production of West Side Story, I greatly **improved my communication and teamworking** skills through **leading** rehearsals in the absence of the director, as well as **developing my time management and organisational skills** by balancing rehearsals with numerous other commitments.'*

Key point

Rather than making sweeping, general statements about yourself, try to imply your skills and experience by going into specific detail. For instance, instead of stating *'I am a dedicated and committed individual'*, a much more effective sentence would be *'Giving up breaks and lunch times to rehearse for the school play required a strong sense of commitment and dedication to my fellow performers.'*

How to turn something mundane into a positive

In the highly competitive world of university applications, it is a truism that how you say something is **almost** as important as what you say. Of course, no matter how voluminous your vocabulary or accomplished you are in the art of writing, stylistic excellence can never compensate for a lack of substance. However, it is equally important to consider the fact that the impact and momentum of your Personal Statement can be utterly stemmed by dull and unconvincing phrasing. For example, consider this sentence:

> *'I have played the drums in a band for three years.'*

I'm sure you'll agree that this is a bland, unremarkable and frankly uninspiring statement of fact. Now consider how we can bolster this sentence with buzz words, in order to compel and convince the reader, and also with reflection, in order to demonstrate that this experience has developed the person concerned. For the purposes of the example, buzz words are highlighted in bold, and reflection is underlined, although you should not use any formatting when writing your Personal Statement:

> *'Having played the drums in a band for the past three years, <u>I have</u> **developed** <u>the ability to work within a team to achieve mutual goals.</u> Through regular rehearsals I have **honed** <u>my communication skills and</u> **demonstrated** <u>great commitment, as well as</u> **enhancing** <u>my time management and organisational abilities</u> through booking gigs and **actively** promoting our band.'*

In the second example, the student did not merely make a statement of fact, but stressed what qualities the activity in question demonstrated about them, as well as reflecting on how the activity has improved them as a person. Crucially, all the buzzwords and reflection also demonstrate that the student is equipped, suitable and prepared for the rigours of studying at university. No matter what you choose to introduce into your Personal Statement, ensure that you relate it to your suitability for studying at university in general, and your chosen course in particular. Again, consider this example:

> *'I have worked in a shop, mainly stacking shelves.'*

Oh dear. Hardly an elite young mind on display! Still, using the principles already mentioned, the student improved this sentence considerably:

> *'When working in a retail environment I **worked hard** to ensure excellent levels of customer service by dealing with customer queries and merchandising the shop floor to a high standard. I also had overall **responsibility** for my own section, and greatly **developed** my communication and interpersonal skills through regular interaction with customers.'*

However, as with any information you choose to include in your Personal Statement, ensure that it is relevant to the skills and aptitudes you will require for your chosen course. Whilst the above example of shop work allowed us to demonstrate the principle of how to turn something mundane into a positive, it is unlikely that you will want to include similar information (unless, of course, your degree is concerned with some aspect of Retail or Hospitality). In a similar vein, if you have had to face setbacks or overcome challenges in recent years, such as underperforming in exams, then you should take the opportunity to reflect on how you have learned from these disappointments and developed as a result of your negative experiences. A good example of how to phrase this in your Personal Statement might be:

> *'Suffering from ME enabled me to develop strategies to cope with setbacks, and reaffirmed my determination to pursue a scientific career.'*

The dirty dozen: Most common mistakes

Despite the fact that the Personal Statement is one of, if not **the** most important aspect of your UCAS application, it's surprising how many applicants submit a poorly structured, meandering and generally lacklustre Personal Statement. With this in mind, we have compiled a list of things to avoid at all costs when planning and writing your Personal Statement:

1. **Length**
    Although you must not exceed 4,000 characters and 47 lines, it is almost as important not to fall too short of these numbers. Coming in at below 3,000 characters will hardly give the impression that you are bursting with enthusiasm or that you have dedicated sufficient time to writing your Personal Statement.

2. **Lack of structure**
    Your Personal Statement must be well planned, logically structured (p. 41) and focused on affirming your suitability for your chosen course. We have all experienced the frustration of listening to someone ramble on as they attempt to explain something to us; do not frustrate the admissions tutors by rambling in your Personal Statement.

3. **Grammar and spelling**

In such a highly competitive arena as university admissions, acceptance or rejection could well be determined by a few sloppy mistakes. Make sure your Personal Statement is proofread several times, and by different people.

4. **Reader-unfriendly**

It is imperative that your Personal Statement is presented in a logical structure, with an opening paragraph explaining why you want to study your chosen course, a main section touching on your academic ability, work experiences and extra-curricular activities, and a concluding paragraph. Simply lumping everything together in one block of uninviting text, with no logical flow of ideas, will not endear you to the admissions tutors. Similarly, it is advisable to vary the length of your sentences, although guard against excessively long, multi-clause sentences. Ideally, you shouldn't require any more than two or three commas: the more commas, the more likely the reader is to get confused or lose the thread of the sentence.

5. **Tone**

It is important to strike an engaging, original tone which reflects your personality. Try to avoid writing in the passive voice. Also, unless you are very confident in your capacity for wit and endearing humour, steer clear of cracking jokes. If you feel a pressing need to use an exclamation mark, do so sparingly, at the very most just once:

> *'The opportunity to witness live surgery during my work experience at Guys and St. Thomas' hospital confirmed that I have the stomach to study medicine!'*

6. **Lack of reflection**

You may be a high achiever, with extra-curricular achievements coming out of your...ahem, ears, but simply describing them is practically pointless without adequate reflection. For example, rather than merely stating that you captained your school hockey team, you need to reflect on the team working, leadership and communication skills you developed as a result of this.

7. **Lack of detail**

Your statement is far more likely to ring true and convince the admissions tutors if you are specific at all times. Vague, sweeping statements such as *'I have always loved to read'* could be made by any Tom, Dick or Harry. In this case, you need to specify your reading habits, and talk about how certain books have stoked your interest in certain themes. Rather than make assertions about yourself, or sweeping statements about how you are *'Motivated, with excellent communication and organisational skills'*, you should seek to substantiate any claims you make for yourself with specific examples.

8. **Stretching the truth**

As tempting as it might seem to embellish the odd assertion here or there, it is seriously inadvisable to lie in your statement. If you are called to interview, it is likely that you will be asked to expand on everything contained in your statement, which will prove an uncomfortable, not to say disastrous experience if you have lied about anything.

9. **Under/overselling**

Avoid negative language:

> *'Despite **failing** to lead my group to victory in a Young Enterprise debating competition...'*

Similarly, do not make grand, hyperbolic assertions about yourself:

> *'With **peerless** organisational skills and an **unrivalled** ability to assimilate new ideas...'*

The admissions tutors will make judgements over your relative merits and abilities based on the information you give and the manner in which you reflect on it. Asserting your own brilliance is highly inadvisable, and will demonstrate little except an overbearing arrogance.

10. **Less is more**

As over-used as this old adage may be, it definitely rings true when it comes to university Personal Statements. There are two main reasons why it is preferable to opt for a concise style of writing: firstly, because doing so will enable you to include more information and reflection before reaching the 4,000 character limit, but also because an excessively florid, overly verbose style stands a greater chance of either confusing or annoying the reader!

- Instead of overwriting…*'As a direct consequence of my active and tireless involvement in school musical productions, whereby I successfully co-ordinated intensive rehearsals and led the band through three brilliantly received performances, I have successfully developed and honed a series of transferable skills, particularly in terms of collaborative working, time management and leadership.'*

- … Or using your statement to showcase your vocabulary… *'My assiduous work as the musical director for school plays such as 'Grease', elicited copious praise from everyone involved, and enabled me to develop a veritable cornucopia of aptitudes, paramount among which being the ability to motivate people towards achieving a mutual goal.'*

- … Aim to convey what you want to say in a clear and concise, yet convincing manner: *'In my role as the musical director for a number of drama club productions at school, I gave up two evenings a week to organise and lead band rehearsals. This required great commitment, as well as the ability to lead a team and communicate effectively. This experience was immensely rewarding and taught me the value of collaborative working.'*

Notice how clumsy and drawn-out the first example is. By cramming in too many ideas and clauses, it makes for a rather difficult read. The second example gives the impression of arrogance – attempting to impress by entering into 'thesaurus mode' is actually far more likely to irritate the reader. Let's face it – it amounts to little more than showing off.

11. **Needless repetition**

    After completing your first draft, it is likely that you will struggle to edit information in order to dip below the 4,000 character limit. One sure fire way of wasting space is to repeat information which is already contained in other sections of your application, for instance by listing your A level subjects and predicted grades.

12. **Me, myself and I**

    Do not start every sentence with 'I'. Don't worry if you find that you have done just that after re-reading your first draft, it is actually the best way of getting your thoughts down on paper. However, when the time comes to redraft your statement, think about how to vary the openings of sentences in order to keep the reader interested and impress with your written style (for ideas, see page 67).

Key points

Be enthusiastic.

Be specific.

Be honest.

Be relevant and truthful.

Chapter 8
From 'Draft' to 'Refined'

From 'Draft' to 'Refined'

An example to consider

Before you begin to write your Personal Statement, consider the two examples below. There are two versions: a 'Draft' and a 'Refined' version. Read through these two versions and the accompanying commentary; you will be taken step by step through how the 'Draft' version has been greatly improved and transformed into the 'Refined' version.

Personal Statement: Draft

I like reading so I would really like the chance to study english at university. I really like horror stories so I would appreciate the chance to learn more about them. I also liked war poetry. Eventually, I am thinking of becoming a journalist, after being inspired by a lecture by Kate Adie that I attended recently.

I think English is a fascinating subject which will really motivate me at university level. I am a keen member of the school debate team and it was a great honour to be made President in 2008. I am also in the hockey team at school and this has given me the opportunity to meet lots of people and has improved my teamwork. I have also been in the swimming and athletics teams, and was in the Junior Choir until Year 9. I went on a French exchange in Year 10 that was really challenging but a good experience. We stayed in a small town outside of Lille, and it improved my speaking skills a lot because it was the only way through which we could communicate.

At the weekends, I work in a local supermarket. I have worked there for two years and get on well with my manager. I have had to become competent at operating a till, and my experience in dealing with customers has been great. There have been a number of occasions where I have had to defuse a situation where a customer has been annoyed, and as a result of my work, I was made Employee of the Week.

I am in the process of completing my Duke of Edinborough Gold Award, and it is a very challenging experience. I am really looking forward to gaining my award, as it has required me to do lots of different activities

such as expeditions, working as a teaching assistant in a local primary school, and learning the piano.

Character count: 1,379

Personal Statement: Refined

Ever since I discovered a love of reading during a lengthy hospital stay at the age of nine, I have often found pleasure in books and this passion has continued to the present day. As a result of my keen interest, I have read a wide range of genres and this has fuelled my desire to study English at a higher level. The modernist writers particularly intrigue me and I would like the opportunity to learn more about the connection between form and content. I also find gothic writing fascinating and I particularly relished Mary Shelley's 'Frankenstein.' With regards to theoretical viewpoints, I have recently been introduced to the theories of Judith Butler. Her concepts of gender and sexuality are stimulating but complex and I would appreciate the chance to study them further in a supported environment. Studying English at university would offer me the opportunity to broaden my literary horizons, whilst expanding my ability to interpret a text.

Recently I attended a lecture by journalist Kate Adie about the responsibilities entailed with journalism. It revealed the extent of the power that the media possesses, something that I found fascinating, and it introduced me to a possible future career path. Through reading the broadsheet newspapers I have gained a greater comprehension of current affairs and have also been able to expand my vocabulary. The benefits of this can be seen in my academic marks.

Participating in the school debating team allowed me to develop my powers of rhetoric and required me to construct convincing and persuasive arguments. This can only be an asset to my studies as constructing a solid argument is imperative to any essay. My success in this field was recognised when I was appointed President of the Debate Team in 2008. This position of responsibility necessitated much organisation on my part; I had to arrange our meetings, put forward topics for debate and ensure that we were fully prepared for all inter-school competitions. Through this role I learnt that effective communication skills are essential, and the confidence I gained through public speaking is invaluable and something I would actively seek to continue at university.

I am currently completing my Duke of Edinburgh Gold Award, which has required me to complete a 50 kilometre expedition in Wales. The expedition stretched my ability to work in a team, particularly under stressful situations, and I now feel confident in my ability to do so. The Duke of Edinburgh Award has also enabled me to work as a teaching assistant in a local primary school. This challenging experience has allowed me to work with small groups of children to improve their literacy skills. I find it very rewarding to follow their improvement, particularly when we can make reading into an enjoyable activity rather than a chore. I am also in the school hockey team and this has afforded me the opportunity to make new friends whilst representing my school. I would hope to continue this at university.

In finishing, I feel I have demonstrated how much I would fully appreciate the opportunities that would be available to me at university, both academically and socially. The chance to enrich my knowledge of the English canon excites me and I do not intend to waste it. By participating fully in university life I hope to reach my full potential.

Character count: 2,788

Enhancing your Personal Statement

This section aims to help you avoid some of the common pitfalls made when writing Personal Statements. By considering the 'Draft' and 'Refined' paragraphs side by side, we can analyse the benefits of the 'Refined' version whilst simultaneously giving you some practical examples of what to avoid.

Paragraph one: Draft

'I like reading so I would really like the chance to study english at university. I really like horror stories so I would appreciate the chance to learn more about them. I also liked war poetry. Eventually, I am thinking of becoming a journalist, after being inspired by a lecture by Kate Adie that I attended recently.'

Paragraph one: Refined

'Ever since I discovered a love of reading during a lengthy hospital stay at the age of nine, I have often found pleasure in books and this passion has continued to the present day. As a result of my keen interest, I have read a wide range of genres and this has fuelled my desire to study English at a higher level. The modernist writers particularly intrigue me and I would like the opportunity to learn more about the connection between form and content. I also find gothic writing fascinating and I particularly relished Mary Shelley's 'Frankenstein.' With regards to theoretical viewpoints, I have recently been introduced to the theories of Judith Butler. Her concepts of gender and sexuality are stimulating but complex and I would appreciate the chance to study them further in a supported environment. Studying English at university would offer me the opportunity to broaden my literary horizons, whilst expanding my ability to interpret a text.'

Paragraph one: Draft

This is not a very attention-grabbing first sentence and it does not inspire confidence in the applicant's love of the subject. Furthermore, vague comments about particular areas you are interested in do not make the most of what you know about your subject. Ensure that you assign a capital letter to subjects i.e. English not english. There is no justification for the reasons that the applicant likes horror stories and war poetry, and no indication of any real reason to become a journalist. Even worse, the applicant seems to be 'name-dropping' Kate Adie into the Personal Statement without even mentioning what they found inspiring. The whole paragraph seems vague and drifting. By starting most sentences with 'I', the applicant shows a lack of written style, and this makes for a boring and uninspired Personal Statement.

Paragraph one: Refined

By emphasising the enjoyment and interest in the subject since childhood, the applicant clearly presents a logical justification for their choice of degree. This is continued with some detailed, thoughtful comments about particular areas the applicant would like to explore in further detail. Now is the chance to show off what you have learnt from your studies so far. If you have conducted some research around the course then make use of this: use technical words specific to your subject to prove to the reader that you are sufficiently keen. Whether this involves mentioning form and content for English, trigonometry and chaos theory for Mathematics or Booker T Washington's theory of black double consciousness for American Studies, show that you have done your homework. The applicant states succinctly what studying their chosen course at university will offer them. The variety of sentence structure and length shows a sophisticated style that will entertain the reader and display the applicant in the best possible light.

Paragraph two: Draft

'I think English is a fascinating subject which will really motivate me at university level. I am a keen member of the school debate team and it was a great honour to be made President in 2008. I am also in the hockey team at school and this has given me the opportunity to meet lots of people and has improved my teamwork. I have also been in the swimming and athletics team, and was in the Junior Choir until Year 9. I went on a French exchange in Year 10 that was really challenging but a good experience. We stayed in a small town outside of Lille, and it improved my speaking skills a lot because it was the only way through which we could communicate.'

Paragraph two: Refined

'Recently I attended a lecture by journalist Kate Adie about the responsibilities entailed with journalism. It revealed the extent of the power that the media possesses, something that I found fascinating, and it introduced me to a possible future career path. Through reading the broadsheet newspapers I have gained a greater comprehension of current affairs and have also been able to expand my vocabulary. The benefits of this can be seen in my academic marks.'

Paragraph two: Draft

The applicant begins a new paragraph by regurgitating much of what has been said in the previous paragraph. Try to ensure that all your sentences follow on from each other but do not repeat what has already been said. The mention of the debate team and the school hockey team is not linked in with the rest of the paragraph and therefore appears disjointed. The applicant makes no attempt to mention any of the responsibilities involved with the role of President or any of the skills they have acquired. Instead there is an attempt to include everything that the applicant has participated in at school. The references to swimming, athletics and junior choir should be omitted as they are no longer relevant and the space could be used for more valuable and recent achievements. The reference to the French exchange trip is, again, irrelevant to the application, and it does not deserve the amount of space apportioned to it. The language and style is still clumsy, and the applicant does not make the most of their achievements.

Paragraph two: Refined

The paragraph starts with a fresh topic, but one that is still very much related to the one before. By mentioning the lecture, the applicant appears to be enthusiastic and motivated. In providing a specific concept that they found interesting the applicant clearly presents us with the insights they have gained. The inclusion of the fact that they read a broadsheet newspaper shows an awareness of current affairs, but also an awareness of the qualities needed to succeed at university, such as a good vocabulary.

Paragraph three: Draft

'At the weekends, I work in a local supermarket. I have worked there for two years and get on well with my manager. I have had to become competent at operating a till, and my experience in dealing with customers has been great. There have been a number of occasions where I have had to defuse a situation where a customer has been annoyed, and as a result of my work, I was made Employee of the Week.'

Paragraph three: Refined

'Participating in the school debating team allowed me to develop my powers of rhetoric and required me to construct convincing and persuasive arguments. This can only be an asset to my studies as constructing a solid argument is imperative to any essay. My success in this field was recognised when I was appointed President of the Debate Team in 2008. This position of responsibility necessitated much organisation on my part; I had to arrange our meetings, put forward topics for debate and ensure that we were fully prepared for all inter-school competitions. Through this role I learnt that effective communication skills are essential, and the confidence I gained through public speaking is invaluable and something I would actively seek to continue at university.'

Paragraph three: Draft

The applicant did not make the most of their achievements within the school debate team by merely mentioning it in the previous paragraph. It would have been better to talk about this one achievement in greater detail, than to include all the other activities they have tried briefly at school. Instead, the applicant wastes a whole paragraph by talking about a part-time job that is in no way relevant to their application. The details mentioned are trivial, and there is no mention of anything that could be useful to their degree. Do not make the mistake of thinking that just because an activity consumes a lot of your time, it warrants the equivalent amount of space in your Personal Statement.

Paragraph three: Refined

The applicant states what their role in the debate team required, and then makes this relevant to their chosen degree. The mention of taking on the role of President is made more impressive by the inclusion of what the role entailed, and also what they have learnt from it. The reader is also made to feel that this is someone who intends to actively contribute to university life through their desire to continue this hobby at university. The style remains well-written; the applicant repeats neither the content nor the words used, ensuring that the sentences are well linked and logical.

Paragraph four: Draft

'I am in the process of completing my Duke of Edinborough Gold Award, and it is a very challenging experience. I am really looking forward to gaining my award, as it has required me to do lots of different activities such as expeditions, working as a teaching assistant in a local primary school, and learning the piano.'

Paragraph four: Refined

'I am currently completing my Duke of Edinburgh Gold Award, which has required me to complete a 50 kilometre expedition in Wales. The expedition stretched my ability to work in a team, particularly under stressful situations, and I now feel confident in my ability to do so. The Duke of Edinburgh Award has also enabled me to work as a teaching assistant in a local primary school. This challenging experience has allowed me to work with small groups of children to improve their literacy skills. I find it very rewarding to follow their improvement, particularly when we can make reading into an enjoyable activity rather than a chore. I am also in the school hockey team and this has afforded me the opportunity to make new friends whilst representing my school. I would hope to continue this at university.'

Paragraph four: Draft

The incorrect spelling of Edinburgh shows, at best, someone who does not take care in their work and, at worst, someone who has poor spelling! Make sure that all spelling and grammar is correct; small mistakes will make a big (and bad) impression. The language is unadventurous, and the applicant rushes through things in a list-like fashion, which minimises the importance and impact of their achievements.

Paragraph four: Refined

As shown previously, the applicant clearly tells us the requirements of the Duke of Edinburgh Award and the knowledge and experience they have gained through participation in the scheme. The specific mention of voluntary work as a teacher's assistant can be linked back to the choice of degree and the applicant's passion for reading.

This sort of paragraph, towards the end of the Personal Statement (although it is acceptable to begin a new paragraph if necessary) is also suitable to contain the applicant's extra-curricular achievements. This portrays the applicant as a well-rounded individual, and again points to the contribution they would like to make at university through participating in hockey.

Concluding paragraph: Draft

Does not exist.

Concluding paragraph: Refined

'In finishing, I feel I have demonstrated how much I would fully appreciate the opportunities that would be available to me at university, both academically and socially. The chance to enrich my knowledge of the English canon excites me and I do not intend to waste it. By participating fully in university life I hope to reach my full potential.'

Concluding paragraph: Draft

A concluding paragraph is absolutely imperative in order to leave the reader with your most important reasons for gaining a place at university. It is a huge mistake not to include one, as it will mean that your Personal Statement will tail off, leaving the reader feeling that you have no real focus.

Concluding paragraph: Refined

The start of the paragraph gives a hint that the Personal Statement is nearly finished, giving the reader time to reconsider the points the applicant has made – it may also provide relief for weary admissions tutors! The applicant gives a broader reminder (this is not the time to introduce new information) of the academic **and** social reasons as to why they wish to attend university, thereby emphasising both their academic interest but also their well-rounded personality.

Chapter 9

Overseas and mature students

Overseas and mature students

Overseas students

According to UCAS, over 70,000 overseas students applied to study at a university in the UK in 2004 but only 30,000 applicants were successful in securing a place, a success rate of just 43%. As the number of overseas students wishing to study in the UK continues to increase, the need for a clear and well-structured UCAS application is becoming increasingly important. However, many overseas students wishing to attend a university course in the UK do not have access to a support service to help and guide them to complete the most important part of the UCAS application – the UCAS Personal Statement.

An overseas student's Personal Statement must justify why a university should invest in a student of this type and show that they are enthusiastic and committed to completing the course in question. Without a well-presented UCAS Personal Statement, the chances of realising your dream of securing a place at university are greatly reduced.

Before applying to study at a UK university as an overseas student, you should verify that your qualifications will be accepted by the admissions offices at the institutions to which you are applying. The decision as to the suitability of your credentials will be made by each individual institution, so it is important that you present an exhaustive list of all the qualifications, awards and certificates you have gained to date. You should send copies (but **not** the originals) of all of your certificates and examination results to each higher education institution you are applying to, along with the name and code of your chosen course and your application number. Also, if English is not your first language, you should inform the institutions to which you are applying whether or not the exams you have passed were assessed in English, and include details of any English language tests you have taken, such as the IELTS qualification. It is important to explain exactly why you wish to study in the UK, as well as to demonstrate your communication skills in the English language by mentioning any activities or positions of responsibility you have held. We would urge you to contact the admissions tutors at institutions you intend to apply to in order to obtain specific help and guidance regarding completing your university application.

To give you an idea of how the Personal Statement of an overseas student will differ from that of a UK resident, we have included an example for you to consider and compare with the examples at the end of this guide:

Engineering – Overseas student

'Growing up in China, the impact of major architectural developments on the economic condition of the local area has been readily apparent, with many areas utterly transformed by large scale construction projects. My aim in studying Engineering is to acquire academic and industry experience before returning to China as an engineer in order to contribute to the stabilising of the economy.

My school studies in China have provided a broad base of background knowledge in Science and Humanities and included an introduction to Engineering, which first motivated me to consider careers within this industry. I enjoyed learning the technical skills involved in drawing plans and have always been fascinated with the very large scale projects such as transport systems, complex bridges linking islands and holistic developments of entire communities, with hospitals, schools, shops and homes all being incorporated in one site. The way in which such developments can alter the location gives the engineer a great deal of power, and consequently responsibility. Comparing modern Chinese engineering with traditional approaches, it is clear how quickly this field has advanced and I enjoyed class discussions speculating on possible future configurations of cities. Maths was a favourite topic at school, allowing me to acquire problem solving and lateral thinking skills, which will be key to my future work as an engineer. At school I was awarded the Prize for Overall Achievement three years running, demonstrating my commitment to achieving my academic potential.

As several relatives are involved in a construction company in China I have been fortunate enough to have had the opportunity to shadow people in a number of different roles within this profession. This has given me an overview of the industry and allowed me to contribute to several planning discussions between the engineers which has given me an idea of the range of problems which might be encountered in design. As the project increases in size and complexity, so do the problems which can

be anticipated. The challenge of handling so many issues at once, whilst continuing to progress towards construction, makes a career in this field appeal to my enjoyment of intellectual stimulation.

In China I spent much of my free time practising brush calligraphy and have twice won the Young Calligrapher award for my province. I find this artistry has developed my manual dexterity and attention to detail as well as allowing my creativity to be expressed. Practice takes a significant commitment of time and energy and has enabled me to learn more about Chinese cultural traditions and modern influences on the ancient art of calligraphy. I was also involved in tutoring younger children in this art under the direction of the academy's master. This experience improved my confidence and sense of responsibility as I became effectively a colleague of my teacher, and tutoring and advising young people has developed my communication skills. Since coming to the UK three months ago I have worked in a restaurant serving customers within a team of waiters. This has improved my conversational English and allowed me to learn something of the culture of the country, and to live independently, which will be good preparation for starting at university.

This degree will equip me for a range of careers requiring numerate and articulate graduates with good interpersonal and problem solving skills. My intention, however, is to train as an engineer and eventually to contribute to the development of my country, and I am prepared for the challenges involved in achieving my aim.'

 **Useful websites:**
www.educationuk.org
www.ukcisa.org.uk

Mature students

The loose definition of a mature student is anyone over the age of 21 who wishes to apply to study at a UK university. As a mature student, you might be a little apprehensive that your lack of formal qualifications, or the length of time which has elapsed since you left school, will render your application less appealing to admissions tutors. However, this couldn't be further from the truth. In fact, as someone who has gained valuable life skills, maturity and work experience, you are far more likely to be offered a place at university with, for example, one or two A levels, than an 18-year-old school leaver would be.

The golden rule is to enquire before applying – many universities publish special guidelines for mature students, so it is important to acquire these in order to tailor your Personal Statement accordingly. It may be that you can apply with your existing background and credentials or you may need to complete an Access course. It is also advisable to send your Curriculum Vitae, including your qualifications and employment experience, to each of the institutions to which you are applying, though **not** directly to UCAS. For further information on how to apply as a mature student, visit the UCAS website (www.ucas.com).

Although it is obviously important to mention any qualifications, formal or otherwise, which you have attained, the activities you have undertaken since leaving school are of equal, if not greater interest to admissions tutors. Whether you have decided on a change of career, wish to pursue a long-standing interest, or you are in a position to make the most of your potential now the children have 'flown the nest', the admissions tutors will be most interested in:

- Why you have chosen to enter higher education at this point in your life.
- The reasons behind your subject choice.
- The steps you have taken to confirm that the course you have chosen is the right one for you.
- How you have prepared yourself for the academic rigours of studying for an undergraduate degree.
- How completing your degree will enable you to progress your career.

No matter how many years have passed since you sat your A levels, and regardless of whether you left school at 16 with a clutch of O levels or GCSEs, you need to demonstrate your subject knowledge and, most crucially, your general academic ability to the admissions tutors. It may be that your career has entailed the skills relevant to studying for a degree, such as research and report writing. Also, your Personal Statement is the perfect arena to talk about any courses, part-time or full-time, which you have taken, such as 'Access', 'Foundation' and Open University courses, as well as any post-16 qualifications such as BTEC, HND, AS and A levels.

The principles which will govern your Personal Statement are exactly the same as those which govern the statement of an 18-year-old school leaver – what you choose to include must clearly and unequivocally demonstrate your academic credentials, your ability to live independently and your suitability for studying your chosen subject. You need to relate what you write about to your chosen course, and demonstrate that you are suitable, in terms of both intellect and temperament, to university life. What follows is an example of how a mature student should reflect on their experiences, both personal and career-related, in order to convince the admissions tutors of their suitability:

Midwifery – Mature student

'Finding my previous career unfulfilling, I have chosen to return to education and train to be a midwife as I feel this will offer a rewarding career in which I can use my empathetic nature to make a positive contribution to people's lives. What appeals to me most is the variety of the midwife's job, including the option of working either in a hospital or in the community, and the privileged position of being able to assist a family through pregnancy to birth.

Biology has been one of my favourite subjects within my Access Course as I enjoy learning about human anatomy and physiology. I have also made the most of this opportunity to practise my study skills to ensure I am able to take full advantage of what my degree has to offer. At university I am looking forward to learning general aspects of nursing prior to specialising in Midwifery. Within Midwifery I am particularly interested in the different stages of pregnancy and childbirth and in the psychological factors affecting a healthy pregnancy and successful birth. My Access Course has included two weeks of work experience in a hospital, which was an excellent chance to connect theory with practice and I am very excited about undertaking clinical placements to learn how to care for the mother and family. At college I have enjoyed investigating research projects and learning to assimilate large quantities of information. I am excited about entering Higher Education and look forward to the challenge of continuing to update my knowledge throughout my career.

My employment history has given me many transferable skills which will be useful during my training and future career. As a part-time call centre supervisor for a large Internet Service Provider I manage a team *of seven and deal with the more difficult queries or complaints as they are referred to me. This requires effective interpersonal skills in order to obtain the necessary information from the caller, and to determine and solve their problem. Calls come from people of all ages and levels of ability in English and in IT and I feel my experience of this, as well as my fluency in three languages, will be valuable in multi-ethnic communities. My job frequently involves dealing with angry and unpleasant customers with a calm and professional approach and I am familiar with working in a pressurised environment. As part of the customer service team I also have experience of working well with colleagues and putting personal opinions aside in order to treat everybody with the same professional manner. Through using different software packages to give advice to callers on the helpline, computers are an integral part of my working day and I have also been able to develop good organisational and time management skills.*

Volunteering with the St John Ambulance service, including Advanced First Aid training, has confirmed my enjoyment of working in healthcare. It has also given me some basic medical knowledge and inspired me to learn more. In order to further my experience I will soon be starting a part-time job as a First Aider within St John Ambulance Caring Services. Training with St John has taught me the value of commitment and dedication, as well as providing experience of working in a team to reach common goals. Prior to my most recent job I was employed in customer services by Marks and Spencer. A substantial part of this job was training staff, many of them significantly older than me, on the new computer systems. I enjoyed taking on the responsibility of advising others and having the opportunity to work with different people every day.

My work with the St John Ambulance Service has confirmed that I am suited to a job in the caring profession. As a mature applicant I have had the time to fully research and consider my options and I feel I am particularly suited to Midwifery. My ambition is to work as a qualified midwife within the NHS, making a significant contribution to the provision of high quality patient care, and I feel I have the commitment and motivation required to achieve my goal.'

Key points

Relate your work experience, including relevant and transferable skills such as report writing or copyediting, to the skills you will need to demonstrate whilst studying your chosen course.

Convince the admissions tutors of your ability to cope with the rigours of undergraduate life – mention evening courses, Access courses or any other relevant activities which demonstrate that you have made efforts to prepare yourself for undergraduate study.

Chapter 10
Redrafting and proofreading

Redrafting and proofreading

By now your Personal Statement should have taken shape, and should follow a clear, logical and coherent structure, with every piece of information serving to demonstrate the following:

- Your academic ability
- Your personal qualities
- Your suitability for studying your chosen course

It is often said that great poetry is a combination of the best words in the best order and, whilst your Personal Statement might not quite rival John Keats' 'Ode to a Grecian Urn' or Alexander Pope's 'The Vanity of Human Wishes', it is fair to state that you need to view your statement as a first draft, which will need editing, honing, re-phrasing and fine tuning in order to really wow the admissions tutors. The first thing to mention about the process of re-drafting your statement is that, after writing your first draft, you should leave it for a few days before you return to it with a fresh pair of eyes. Overfamiliarity can blind us to faults. You have no doubt had the experience of proofreading an essay or piece of course work but, only reading what you wanted to see rather than what you actually saw on the the page, you completely missed a glaring error. Go back and re-read the last sentence. The more eagle-eyed amongst you might well have picked up on the deliberate mistake:

'You have no doubt had the experience of proofreading an essay or piece of course work but, only reading what you wanted to see rather than what you actually saw on **the the** page, you completely missed a glaring error'.

Although many of you will not have done. Don't worry if you didn't, it's a classic linguistic trick which demonstrates that our brains often 'see' what they think ought to be there, rather than what actually is. Proofreading your own statement is imperative but it is equally important to ask other people to proof it as well, particularly teachers, parents or older siblings who are at, or have been to university and have had to write a Personal Statement themselves.

It is useful to ask a variety of people to read through your Personal Statement. The opinions of other people will help you to view your Personal Statement from different perspectives. Explain to them the message you are trying to portray through your Personal Statement. A useful tick list for your completed Personal Statement is:

- Do you have a punchy and relatively attention grabbing introduction?
- Do you explain your reasons for choosing your subject?
- Do you state what you are looking forward to learning more about?
- Do you state your future career goals?
- Do you state how your academic and extra-curricular activities have developed you as an individual?
- Is the information you provide relevant to your chosen course?
- Is your Personal Statement arranged in paragraphs?
- Does your Personal Statement contain a short concluding paragraph?

For further ideas on improving your first draft in terms of style, phrasing and buzzwords, see page 64.

Chapter 11

Information for teachers and parents

Chapter 11

Information for teachers and parents

In a sense, the hardest aspect of writing a Personal Statement is staring at a blank piece of paper and actually beginning the process. The best way to help someone who is struggling to get to grips with their Personal Statement is to talk through their academic and personal achievements with them, and encourage them to think about the skills and personality traits they have developed and which they are particularly proud of. If a young person is finding it difficult to be enthusiastic about the prospect of writing a university Personal Statement, first encourage them to enthuse about their hobbies and pastimes in open discussion, and use this as a springboard to launching into the 'thought showering' process. For ideas on getting started, see the section of this guide on 'Gathering ideas' (p. 39).

Possible areas to discuss with an applicant include:

- Topics they have particularly enjoyed learning about whilst studying for their A levels. Why did they enjoy this area – what skills did it allow them to demonstrate and develop? (i.e. a History project enabled them to discover their enjoyment of researching in a library, or studying 'group theory' in Psychology has given them new insights into their relationships at school).
- Career aims – what areas are they considering a career in? What subjects do they think would provide a gateway to a career in their chosen field?
- What achievements, both in and out of school, are they particularly proud of? How has participating in these activities developed them as a person?

Once a young person has drafted their first attempt at their Personal Statement, you can help them further by proofreading it and offering constructive criticism. For ideas on how to improve a first draft, see our chapter on 'Writing tips' (p. 64). In addition, consider their first draft in the light of the following checklist:

- Does it contain a punchy and relatively attention grabbing introduction?
- Does it explain their reasons for choosing their subject?
- Does it state what they are looking forward to learning more about?
- Does it state their future career goals?
- Does it state how their academic and extra-curricular activities have developed them as an individual?
- Is the information included relevant to their course choice?
- Is the Personal Statement arranged in paragraphs?
- Does the Personal Statement contain a short concluding paragraph?

Chapter 12

Further reference: Personal Statement examples

Further reference: Personal Statement examples

Here follows a series of successful Personal Statements which cover a range of subjects and university courses. When reading them, bear in mind that they have been subjected to a similar process of refinement and redrafting as outlined in this guide, so you should not feel too concerned that your own first draft will fall short of the standard on display. In fact most, if not all of the following statements were somewhat average at the first draft stage, and it was only through a concerted process of refining and restructuring that they were eventually moulded into high-quality Personal Statements.

Please note that these examples, together with other examples referred to throughout this guide, are for guidance purposes only and should not be used as part of your university application.

Accounting

Example 1

My motivation to study Accounting to degree level springs from my enjoyment of Business Studies AS level; being able to gain such a variety of different perspectives on the business world has showed me the unlimited professional opportunities available. My coursework case studies have given me an insight into the complexities involved in operating a wide range of different types of business, something I found most intriguing; particularly those which relate to any financial considerations. Business Studies AS level has allowed me to focus my academic attentions on the area of business that fascinates me the most: Accountancy. Studying Accountancy to degree level will allow me to explore, in depth, a range of stimulating and interdisciplinary topics, which I feel will give me a broader understanding towards the theories and practices of management in different organisations in relation to a financial environment.

I feel that my skills, attributes and existing business knowledge are particularly suited to a career in Accountancy. My communication skills have been enhanced through my part-time employment, where my promotion to weekend footwear manager is enabling me to develop knowledge of financial record keeping, problem solving, meeting weekly sales targets and teamwork awareness. I feel these skills can be used and put into practice whilst studying my preferred degree course. My AS Business course has given me an understanding of organisations as a whole, but experiences such as working on our Yearbook and running the school stationery shop have really enabled me to expand my knowledge and consciousness of such financial topics through practical application of my skills. My competence in ICT has developed highly through studying it at A Level; a skill I feel is invaluable within the business field. The main thing I have learnt from all my experience, both in school and extra-curricular, is that for all businesses, financial matters are imperative; it is the core of any organisation and being knowledgeable in such issues attracts me.

At school, I have participated in many fund-raising events, open days and further education fairs. From the age of seven I have attended a judo club and have competed at County, Regional and National levels. The feeling I got when I played a role within the team to gain the gold medal was amazing, equal to the feeling when I achieved an individual gold medal as the top National all-round competitor. The realisation of how important managing school work with a physically and emotionally demanding hobby has given me an understanding of how to be realistic, a skill which is valuable when planning certain business strategies.

I believe that during my Sixth Form studies I have grown in both confidence and maturity, preparing me for the opportunity to study at university. My choice of AS and A levels, along with other academic and personal achievements, have helped to consolidate and support my desire to study Accountancy at degree level. I will be fully committed to successfully completing my degree and relish any opportunities which are given to help me achieve my aspirations in a business related career.

Example 2

Accounting and Finance play a crucial role in the effective management of any successful business. Having studied Maths at A level I have been fascinated to explore the role of accountancy in analysing, modelling, mapping and reporting aspects of a company's finances and devising strategies for future development. Given my ultimate intention of returning to China to pursue a career as an accountant, I am keen to gain the level of expertise required to make a significant contribution to China's rapidly developing business sector.

At college I have proven my talent for topics rooted in advanced mathematical techniques and I have enjoyed studying the range of applications of mathematical and statistical maths within Accounting and Finance. Throughout my A levels I have enjoyed rising to new challenges and particularly the opportunities I have had to discuss and debate issues arising in class with fellow students. Since coming to Ireland in order to increase my opportunities I have benefited from an educational system that encourages students to explore their academic interests and develop their individual talents. In undertaking undergraduate study in the UK, I hope to continue to take advantage of a world-respected level of education. This will also enable me to experience a different aspect of European culture and to further enhance my English language skills. During my degree I am particularly looking forward to studying Corporate Finance as this will develop my insight into investments, shares, options and other financial instruments. I am fascinated by the use of ratio calculations to assess whether a company is a worthwhile investment and to predict possible returns and I feel this would be a useful skill for the future. Issues such as Market Efficiency have also interested me at undergraduate level and I am keen to pursue these topics further.

Coming to Ireland and adapting to a new life here, familiarising myself with the culture and language and building a new network of friends and colleagues, has played a significant role on my personal growth. My eyes have been opened to different ways of life and it has been a wonderful opportunity for me to come to Ireland and study in a totally different culture. Despite the challenges associated with making such a move at the age of 18, I feel that this is the most effective way of strengthening one's personality and it has been an immensely rewarding experience. Alongside academic and language skills, I have developed a confident, open minded and flexible approach to life and have had the opportunity to explore my love of different cultures and traditions.

At college I enjoyed contributing to the student body as committee member for the Arts Club, interviewing freshmen who were interested in singing, dancing, and drama. I also helped to organise the college open day, festivals, the graduate ceremony and other big events on campus. Arranging the practice schedules involved co-ordinating students from different faculties with different timetables and required effective time management, interpersonal and organisational skills. In leisure time I enjoyed playing on the college's successful volleyball team and continue to keep fit through swimming and playing table tennis. Photography allows me a creative outlet and I also enjoy travelling and exploring new areas of the world.

After graduating from my degree I would like to complete a postgraduate qualification and gain industry experience before returning to China to continue my career. As a resourceful, ambitious and committed student I am confident that I have a lot to offer the degree programme and I look forward to the challenges and rewards it represents.

Actuarial

Example 3

My motivation to apply for Actuarial Science at university is the desire to study a subject that will combine my interests in Maths and Business Studies, and that has real life applications in the business world. At university I hope to gain the mathematical and analytical skills for a successful career as an actuary when I graduate.

Whilst studying Maths I have enjoyed learning how to manipulate and understand numbers and mathematical concepts, and through my other A levels I have seen that the principles of maths are fundamental to the sciences and economic aspects of business. In particular, I enjoy the modules we have completed on Mechanics, as these principles are visible in action in everyday life. For my Business Studies coursework I completed an investigation into the retail company Marks and Spencer in which I assessed the reasons for their fall in profits and possible ways in which their profitability could be improved. Working on this project gave me a good understanding of how a large business is run at different levels and of the factors which can influence its profits. In particular, I found the freedom of carrying out self-directed research very motivating and I am looking forward to taking increased responsibility for my own learning when I progress to university. My A level in Linguistics has also been interesting and studying aspects of sociolinguistics, such as how we change our language in different professional or personal situations, has helped to improve my own communications skills. The coursework module was again my favourite component. I was able to choose an area of great interest to me, first language acquisition, collect data from the Reception class of a local primary school, and read about relevant theories in my own time.

At university I am looking forward to gaining the skills to evaluate, analyse and solve financial problems and social issues that are rooted in the economic world. I also intend to take advantage of the opportunity to gain experience of the actuarial industry through summer placements during my degree and to take the necessary exams to advance within the actuarial profession upon graduation. At school I have been involved in the Duke of Edinburgh Award scheme and I am now working towards my Gold award, which I will obtain whilst at university. Fulfilling the requirements of the Bronze and Silver awards has exposed me to new hobbies and interests, such as learning the saxophone and playing with a jazz quartet.

I have also enjoyed developing my leadership skills whilst contributing to the community. Through the co-ordinating of a team of befrienders at a local old people's home, I fulfilled the volunteering part of the award. For each expedition I have taken part in, I have played a key role in organising the trip and planning our team's training and preparations. At the moment we are organising a two-week hiking expedition in Bavaria, for the Gold Award, and I have taken responsibility for organising all of the travel and accommodation, with the guidance of my teachers.

In the future my aim is to qualify as an actuary and to work in the industry, although I am also considering further postgraduate study in a specialist area before beginning my career. I am a hard working and disciplined student and I am looking forward to the challenges and opportunities of university study.

Example 4

Having worked as a secretary and receptionist for an actuarial firm for several years, I now wish to train in this field in order to qualify and practice as an actuary myself. After leaving school I decided to go straight into employment for financial reasons, but I now have the confidence, ambition and financial security to return to education and develop my career. Although I have not approached this degree through the conventional route, I feel confident that I have the academic ability and motivation to be a successful student.

As a secretary and receptionist I have supported the work of the actuaries in my firm for eight years and have found it a fascinating and varied profession to be involved in. My work involves taking calls from current and prospective clients, maintaining records on computer and hard copy, writing and responding to letters and emails on behalf of the actuaries, and assisting them as required. Through this I have gained a good understanding of the types of work taken on by actuaries and have learnt the basic processes of assessing risk management in monetary terms. My company are supportive of my decision to retrain and I have decided to study part time so that I can continue to work. This real life experience of actuarial work will provide me with a context to my studies, helping me to quickly make sense of the theories and techniques I will study, and will give me a lot to contribute to class discussions.

In order to prepare myself for university I have spent the last two years studying an Undergraduate diploma through a distance learning course with the Open University. This has included two residential schools which have given me a taste of student life and I have enjoyed attending monthly tutorials and weekly study group meetings to support my home-based study. Studying from home requires a great deal of organisation of time and resources and will have prepared me well for co-ordinating my degree with my job. University level study has been a steep learning curve but I am now familiar with current literature in Maths and Science, with using the internet and libraries for research, writing reports and completing problem-based assignments within tight deadlines. I found the module on Mathematical Methods and Models to be particularly interesting, as it focuses on real life problems and different methods of solution using algebra, differential equations, calculus and matrices as well as traditional numerical methods. As well as the residential school, much of the teaching was delivered online so I am now competent using a computer for most of my studies.

In my leisure time I enjoy long distance walking, and I am the social secretary of the local branch of the Ramblers' Association. This role involves attending regular meetings and organising social and fundraising events for the group, such as quiz nights, local walking festivals and theme parties. This has allowed me to utilise the administrative skills I have gained through my work as a secretary to help benefit a hobby I enjoy promoting. I try to go on one long distance walk each year, and this summer I am planning to complete the Pennine Way, a distance of over 270 miles, a feat which requires fitness, stamina and determination.

In conclusion, I hope that I have demonstrated my academic ability and the commitment I have to achieving my ambition of graduating with a relevant degree and practising as an actuary.

Archaeology

Example 5

Since completing my Year 10 work experience with the West Yorkshire Archaeology service I have been intent on following a career in this field, using scientific techniques to investigate the past. Through completing a degree in Archaeological Science I hope to learn the necessary expertise to analyse and interpret artefacts, and to make a contribution to the understanding of our history.

In Physics A level I have particularly enjoyed completing practical experiments and evaluating their results, understanding the properties of different materials and how they interact with each other. Studying the mechanics behind structures such as bridges has made me consider which parts of our buildings will survive for future archaeologists to find, and demonstrated that when studying historical remains we have to remember that only certain materials will remain. I have also enjoyed experiments in Chemistry and Biology AS level, and learning the theory behind processes such as carbon dating, dendrochronology and palaeontology which allow archaeologists to make sense of the organic material they find. I am fascinated by how these techniques can be used to work out the food ancient people ate, the clothes they wore and the way they lived, and I am keen to learn more about similar theories and how they apply to historical investigation. Studying History has allowed me to develop my essay writing skills as well as to gain an overview of some of the most important events of recent history. In particular I found the module on the rise of Nazism and Fascism interesting, as it was possible to see the similarities between these two movements and how they achieved dominance.

For my work experience I spent three weeks with the archaeology department of my county council, cleaning and labelling artefacts in the storeroom, reading recent research and accompanying staff on site visits. As most of the time was spent surveying sites prior to construction I was able to learn a great deal about the day to day life of an archaeologist. Discussing the subject with the staff, I was surprised to find that material from the Second World War was considered by many to be too recent for archaeological attention, as good written records are available. At university I am looking forward to learning how archaeological expertise can help us to understand the history of the 20th century, such as trench warfare. I am especially interested to learn which areas archaeology can be useful in even when there are written records, such as when providing evidence to support contentious arguments.

As a Student Council Representative my duties have included attending monthly meetings and discussing problems with both staff and students, which has helped to develop my interpersonal skills. Practising for the debating team, and competing in the national finals, has improved my verbal communication and my ability to justify an argument logically. It has also allowed me to travel around the country meeting other pupils and discussing topical issues. I regularly read the broadsheet newspapers as well as magazines such as National Geographic and Time, to help me stay well informed for debates. In my leisure time I also enjoy reading magazines such as History Today and Current Archaeology. In the future I intend to continue studying with a postgraduate qualification, and to gain as much work experience as possible, before beginning a career as an archaeologist. This degree will give me the opportunity to learn the skills and knowledge required, as well as to discover new friends and hobbies, and I am thoroughly looking forward to the challenge of living and studying at university.

Example 6

Archaeology interests me as a subject that makes use of the knowledge and practical techniques of several different disciplines, including history, forensics, biology, chemistry and physics. After several years in a career which I have found unfulfilling I have decided to change direction and return to university to study a subject I love.

For five years I have been an active volunteer with a local conservation society which meets fortnightly to do practical environmental tasks. On several occasions this has included environmental archaeology, such as a recent trip to the cave system underneath MacDuff's Tower in Fife, where recently discovered Pictish drawings are being eroded by the sea. Modern industry and technology is powerful enough to destroy, in a few seconds, artefacts which have been preserved for millennia, so I feel it is now more important than ever to preserve such remains, to help ourselves and future generations learn about the past. Through the conservation society I have met several archaeologists and have been able to learn about their typical working day and the requirements of their training. Since deciding to embark on this change of career I have also spent a week shadowing an archaeological consultant at work and on site visits, observing him take notes and assess sites of possible historic interest, write reports and evaluate cases. I also spent some time in the storehouse, cleaning pottery fragments from a recent excavation with the appropriate brushes and bagging the fragments according to size.

For the last two years I have been taking several courses of study at a local college and through distance learning. Re-sitting my Physics and Chemistry A levels has ensured I have the appropriate background knowledge and I have also been studying Open University short courses in Environmental Science, British History and Archaeology. This has introduced me to the relevant subjects and also ensured I am prepared for tertiary level study. In Archaeology I have enjoyed following debates on current issues such as how to limit the archaeological damage to war zones such as Iraq, and whose responsibility this should be. During my degree I look forward to continuing to discuss such issues with

like-minded students and to following my particular interests, such as by studying the relationship between politics and archaeology, marine archaeology and conservation.

My work as a receptionist has equipped me with many useful skills and experiences that will be transferable both to my future career and life as a student. Dealing with the public every day by telephone, email, post and in person, has given me excellent interpersonal skills and confidence in communicating with people at all levels. As I am part of a team with group targets to reach, I am also familiar with working cooperatively with others to achieve cohesive teamwork. As a mother I have experience of using time management to prioritise the many demands on my time, and will continue to do so throughout my degree. In my leisure time I enjoy taking my family on days out to historic buildings, particularly ancient structures such as stone circles, as well as cycling and playing tennis. I enjoy an active life and intend to involve myself fully at university. Having given up my job in order to concentrate on pursuing my dream of becoming an environmental archaeologist, I am fully committed to making a success of my new career and to taking full advantage of the opportunities available to me at university.

Architecture

Example 7

In studying Architecture I hope to gain entry to a career which combines academic, creative and practical skills and has the potential to have a significant impact on the socio-economic development of communities. My Maths and Physics A levels have provided me with analytical and research skills, as well as a basic understanding of the principles of mechanics which are relevant to design and construction. My DT course however, has been particularly stimulating for me and I wish to continue this blend of applied imagination and manual dexterity during my degree. Following my ideas through from initial draft plans to evaluation of their success after the final construction has been very rewarding.

Travelling around Europe, I have had the opportunity to discover a variety of architectural styles. The communist architecture of Central and Eastern European cities such as Budapest and Tallinn provides a stark contrast to the earlier styles. The prolific use of imagery designed to glorify the worker, when compared to the focus on religious or imperial iconography of typical 19th century buildings, demonstrates clearly the powerful relationship between architecture and a society's culture and perception. It is also an example of the use of innovative architecture to alter and enhance people's views of an area, as is being practised in numerous regeneration projects across Britain. Visiting Birmingham and Leeds I have been fascinated by the differences brought to these cities, following the current trend of focusing on waterways and the impact they have had in enlivening and rejuvenating the areas. I enjoy following these issues in newspapers and journals and recently I was interested to read an article discussing failed and superficially successful attempts at regeneration, such as in Gateshead, and the possible reasons behind this. In my degree I look forward to the opportunity to debate such issues with students and lecturers who share my enthusiasm.

As Captain of my school football team, and a player on my local side, I have developed the ability to encourage others to play at their best, as well as being a strong team player myself. I train for football five times a week and this commitment of time and energy has been rewarded by our team recently winning the regional under-21 championships. My part-time job at a local factory has given me independence, responsibility and good interpersonal skills as I work with colleagues of all ages.

I have often taken on roles working with other people, such as tutoring lower school students in Science. Working with younger students has taught me patience and improved my leadership skills. Participating in the school committees for organising the Sixth Form prom and designing the yearbook challenged my creative skills, and I intend to get involved in organising events for societies at university. I am eager to learn new skills and acquire knowledge that will assist me in my future career. In the future I hope to practice as an architect working on urban regeneration programmes and I believe I have the qualities required to achieve this goal.

Example 8

The process of adapting artistic ideas for the appearance and structure of a building to its material, social and cultural contexts is a fascinating prospect. Studying Art and Design I have seen how the design element goes beyond simply drawing plans, making critical judgements and logical analysis of the information given to suggest and refine ideas for appropriate buildings. My work experience has confirmed that I wish to practise as an architect in the future.

Studying Music has encouraged my creative expression and I have learnt skills in performance and theory. Through the history components, I have been introduced to the idea of art forms progressing and developing through time, and to the use of historical music as a gateway through which to access the thoughts and identities of past people. In Physics and Chemistry I have developed my skills in both group and self-directed research and I particularly enjoy the opportunity to collate results with others and discuss our findings in order to draw conclusions, as I feel this is an effective way to learn. I am excited by the facilities which will be available to me at university, making use of design studios and workshops, and particularly to using advanced computer laboratories. In my IT AS I enjoyed using basic image manipulation software and I will be very keen to enhance my skills in this direction as I feel making use of IT packages has the potential to have a radical impact on the world of architecture.

Shadowing an architect in a small local firm, I experienced the daily life of a professional in this field and was able to discuss with her some of the range of career paths available. In the course of the two week placement I observed meetings with construction companies to oversee the conversion of a large warehouse building into executive apartments. I was very interested in the architect's views on the importance of renovating disused local buildings for modern purposes, making use of original features and materials as much as possible. I also learnt about local planning restrictions and the health and safety issues associated with working with buildings constructed before such safeguards existed.

As elected Deputy Head Girl at school, my duties include leading a team of Senior Prefects, assisting the Head of Sixth Form, and liaising between staff and students. I have also helped to organise a recycling campaign at school, increasing recycling facilities for example, which has required me to develop strong interpersonal and organisational skills. Conservation and local heritage issues are important to me and over the summer I volunteered to help with delivering information to visitors at a local Country Park. This has enhanced my written communication and IT skills as I have helped to create leaflets and PowerPoint presentations introducing people to different areas of the wildlife site.

As an active and well motivated student I am looking forward to meeting the challenges of university study and making the most of both the academic and creative facilities, so that I can pursue my ambition of a career as an architect specialising in preserving aspects of local culture.

Biochemistry

Example 9

My motivation to study Biochemistry stems from a desire to use my fascination with science and the human body to contribute positively to the community. Work experience has shown me the realities of a career in Biochemistry and given me a passion to better understand the processes which occur every day within the human body.

On graduating from school I received distinctions for Chemistry, Biology and Maths and in 2010 received a credit award for the Chemistry Olympiad. Taking part in the 2011 Genethics competition has been very rewarding as it involves discussing the ethical issues associated with human genetics and submitting an essay exploring a hypothetical scenario. I was judged in the top six in Queensland and was selected to present my essay at the State Finals. After the Finals we visited hospitals and research labs which allowed me to learn about the variety of careers available within the field of Biochemistry. Science summer schools have enhanced this and I particularly enjoyed a lecture by the Nobel Laureate in Medicine, Peter Doherty, on his discoveries within cell mediated immune systems. This was inspiring as it demonstrated the impact one team's efforts could have on so many people in the world.

My work experience at my local hospital, assisting within a team of scientists, gave me a valuable insight into the operation of a working laboratory. This has been an excellent opportunity to learn practical skills in creating and testing samples as well as the need for good communication within the team. Currently I am taking a gap year in order to help care for my grandmother, who was recently diagnosed with lung cancer, as I feel I will learn from her doctors and nurses as well as increasing my practical experience.

As the Science Ambassador I distributed information about current developments in science to the school, improving my communication skills with people of all ages. After election on to the Student Council, I worked in a team to represent students' issues to staff and enjoyed contributing to the school community. Organising the 2011 Harmony Day, to which international students were invited to a special lunch, required my skills in management of time and resources. I have also worked as tutor to Grade 1 pupils, assisting with their schoolwork as part of my Duke of Edinburgh award.

To balance the pressures of studying I enjoy a range of hobbies. I play tennis and the piano, and I have recently taken up fencing. Politics is also important to me and I took part in the School Constitutional Convention in which teams discuss issues such as the committing of troops to Iraq. I was very pleased to be selected for the 2008 Future Experiences in Agriculture, Science and Technology Camp, a residential camp in which teams use ingenuity and initiative to complete problem solving tasks. On the 'Australia's Vanishing Frog' project I camped with a team of ten, collecting data from across New South Wales. Working in residential teams has given me a more mature outlook and allowed me to meet and work with new people from around the world.

My ambition is to become successful in the field of Biochemistry, working to understand the human body and develop ways of helping the community, and as a committed student with an active extra-curricular life, I believe I have the qualities to make a positive contribution to the university and to succeed in my goal.

Example 10

The attraction of studying Biochemistry at degree level is the fact that it is an ever growing subject area; there will always be new biological theories, findings and discussions, and placing myself within the highest level of academic research and facilities will mean that I am exposed to the most exciting and innovative new developments. I have always fostered a keen interest in Biology, specifically Biochemistry, and I believe that studying it to degree level will give me the skills necessary to deepen my understanding of the subject, enhance my existing knowledge and, eventually, provide me with the qualifications necessary for post-graduate study to become a Chiropractor.

This decision was strengthened following treatment for my own back problems and the improvement in my overall health after conventional medicine had failed. It allowed me to understand that whilst Biology is a subject based on scientific fact and actuality, it can also be used in different ways to play a part in a wide variety of new, innovative ideas and theories. Studying a degree in Biochemistry would therefore be an invaluable step towards my own participation in such developments.

Unfortunately work experience in the chiropractic field is extremely difficult to come by and I have been unable to experience any. Instead, I worked for two weeks in a biological sciences laboratory attached to a large branch of a chemist chain. It was yet another example of how Biology can be used in the workplace; it allowed me to experience a very different use for a Biochemistry degree, far removed from human biology or anatomy.

Earlier in the year I attended a Medlink event aimed at informing potential medical candidates of courses available. This reinforced my decision in both my chosen career and the option to take Biochemistry as an undergraduate degree rather than Medicine, as this remains the best way to get into chiropractic study. Aside from this, until recently I have been working at a supermarket on the delicatessen. Although not linked with my course or career,

I felt that the job proved invaluable in the development of my communication skills and being able to work as a team. Due to the nature of the work, I was also constantly working to deadlines.

Whilst I am a very hardworking and conscientious student, I feel it is important to make time for extra-curricular activities. Socialising is especially important to me because it provides an outlet for stress and helps communication, which in my chosen career is extremely valuable. I am a member of Outreach, the school's voluntary community work scheme, through which I have worked with a local special needs school within lessons. I have spent a year at this school, working with the teachers to help the children move around between lessons and making sure they are comfortable in the classroom. Through this job I have learned the value of patience and empathy, two qualities that are very important should I become a Chiropractor.

Despite my numerous out of school activities, I would like to assure that I allow time for my work and never miss deadlines. I am a conscientious worker and my studies have always taken preference over my personal interests and will continue to do so in order to fulfill my future goals. Studying Biochemistry at university will place me at the forefront of new biological developments and ideas and expose me to brilliant facilities and academic minds. It has been a long standing ambition to obtain a degree in Biochemistry, and I cannot wait to begin.

Biology

Example 11

From an early age I have had a fascination with understanding the complex machinery of the human body, and my curiosity has evolved into a determination to pursue a demanding yet satisfying career in Biology.

My enthusiasm was sparked when I joined the St. John Ambulance Service and thoroughly enjoyed participating in a team and learning the basics of First Aid, for which I received a First Level training certificate. The experience drove me on to learn more about how illnesses and injuries affect the human body, how the body works to protect itself against infections and the complex process of healing. Work experience in a local brewery allowed me to experience first-hand the atmosphere of a working laboratory and opened my eyes to the possibilities of a career in the field of Biological sciences and the realities of working in a real laboratory. I thoroughly enjoyed the experience and I now look forward to developing my own scientific career.

A Level Human Biology has given me an in-depth understanding of the body and Chemistry has helped develop my research skills. In Maths I enjoy problem solving and methodical calculations. Recently I went to a two day Biological Sciences symposium at the University of Leeds which expanded my perspective and gave me a taste of student life. My favourite part was participating in research work in the laboratory, where blood was stained then visualised through a light microscope. I will also soon be attending a Medlink conference. The online BMJ and Doctor magazines fascinate me and I regularly keep up-to-date with current issues. To help with scientific terms I have been learning Latin as an extracurricular activity. As I love learning new languages, I am also currently studying German at a different college.

My part-time job at watersotres bookstore enables me to work well in a team and has helped me develop my communication skills and the ability to show empathy towards customers, useful interpersonal skills which I will employ at university. I am currently taking a Bookseller's Diploma to achieve my maximum potential in my work place. Through organising a dinner event I have raised a substantial amount of money in aid of the tsunami victims. I have helped in past charity dinner events too, for example, to raise money for the HeSCA charity fund at the local hospital. Inspired by the Make Poverty History campaign, I am also currently organising a musical festival to raise money for this cause. Fitness is a key element of my life, particularly playing badminton, squash and baseball. I have been playing the guitar for five years and have achieved Grade 7. Writing my own songs, performing in bands, and recording our music has taught me the value of persistence and self motivation in realising my ambitions.

My work experience has taught me that Biology is a demanding field with a number of different challenges and applications. However, I feel that as a well-motivated, enthusiastic, and passionate individual I have the skills and dedication to fulfil the demands of the course and to succeed in my chosen vocation.

Example 12

My motivation to study Biology stems from my deep interest in applied sciences and my wish to utilise this in a role which involves a detailed study of human physiology. Biologists have the opportunity to make discoveries which would make a significant contribution to the community and I would appreciate the challenge of a career which requires lifelong learning.

At present I am enjoying my Access course and particularly the study of the skeletal system in Biology as I am fascinated by the arrangement and function of the bones, the composition of cartilage and bone tissue, and the occurrence and treatment of bone injuries. In Health Science I have found cell types and their different functions in humans, plants and animals extremely interesting. In Chemistry I find satisfaction in balancing equations and have learnt practical research skills carrying out experiments. The problem solving aspect of Maths appeals to me, especially when several techniques have to be applied before an answer can be obtained. My return to education has been an exciting experience allowing me to develop good study skills such as collating group and independent research results, meeting deadlines, and assimilating large quantities of information. I take pride in reading round my subjects and currently am enjoying 'Mastering Biology' by Kilgour and Riley, as well as general Chemistry textbooks.

During my degree I look forward to covering all aspects of Biology and learning how to apply this knowledge specifically to understanding the complexities of the human body. I will benefit greatly from developing my knowledge of physiology and anatomy and I am interested to learn how illnesses and drugs affect different systems of the body. Through college I will be undertaking a work placement at a working laboratory which will give me valuable experience in the realities of a career in this field. I intend to make full use of this opportunity to learn from qualified biologists who have already completed their studies. At university I will make the most of work placements to ensure I have a balance of real life and academic experience.

My employment history has given me many transferable skills which will be useful at university and in my future work. Several years of agency work has given me the flexibility to adapt to different environments and roles, and confidence in working with new colleagues as well as an awareness of my limitations and when to ask for assistance. Working in Records Management Personnel, I acquired excellent organisational, time management, and administrative skills as my duties involved managing company schedules, organising correspondence, maintaining appointments diaries and managing records. In my current position I am a member of the Customer Advice Team at a B&Q store. This role focuses on customer satisfaction and good interpersonal skills are required, as well as the ability to work well in a team environment. Managing my academic work load with my job has demanded effective prioritising and demonstrates my commitment to improving my prospects.

Outside college and work I have a passion for athletics and find regular jogging is an excellent way to unwind and maintain my health. I also attend regular live music gigs, and enjoy learning more about the culture and history of my local area through sightseeing trips. As a mature student I have considered my career options thoroughly and am fully committed to this opportunity to change direction. My ambition is to work as a researcher in the field of Biology, and I feel I have the skills and motivation to achieve this goal.

Biomedical Science

Example 13

In the current climate of scientific and medical research, major advances are made through an interdisciplinary approach. It is this approach to biomedical research that first excited me at college, studying the links between Biology and Chemistry, and has since fuelled my desire to pursue a career as a biomedical research scientist. I am fascinated by the way in which the delicate balance between different biological mechanisms is maintained and the consequences of its failure and I look forward to studying this in more detail as part of a Biomedical Sciences degree.

Through college science projects I learned to apply a disciplined and thoughtful approach to the way in which I planned and carried out my experiments and I enjoyed making a positive contribution to the research activities of the group. My investigations involved the study of the stomach bacterium Helicobacter pylori (H. pylori) and built upon recent evidence that has shown a strong link between H. pylori infection in the stomach and an increased risk of stomach cancer. I found working in a laboratory environment both challenging and rewarding as it offered me the chance to learn new practical and analytical skills and gave me an insight into laboratory-based research. In addition I was motivated to organise my time efficiently and became self-sufficient by working independently when necessary.

These skills have been reinforced and built upon through working as an assistant in a pharmaceutical laboratory in my home country of Libya. This enabled me to experience biomedical research from an industrial perspective and I found this helpful when making my decision to follow a research career in the academic sector rather than the industrial sector. Also, because the company had international links, I was pleased to be able to develop my communication and foreign language skills further, all qualities that will prepare me for the rigorous demands required for undertaking a degree in a foreign country.

I look forward to being able to undertake my undergraduate studies in the UK, not only because of the exceptionally high standard of teaching at university level combined with the internationally recognised research profile the UK enjoys, but also because it would give me the opportunity to expand my cultural horizons and to participate in multicultural social activities and pursuits. As well as enjoying outdoor social sports such as tennis and horse riding, my interests also include computers, reading and socialising. I am keen to meet new people and to get involved in the various activities and clubs the university has to offer. I believe it is important to balance the hard work associated with academic study with relaxation, physical activity and social interaction.

I am convinced that my decision to undertake a degree is the right one and, whilst I acknowledge that the work will be demanding, I am confident that my motivation to succeed and my hard-working nature will ensure that I will rise to each new challenge and overcome each obstacle to achieve my goal. Gaining a degree in a subject I feel so passionate about will equip me with the academic and practical tools I need to progress through my ambition of becoming an accomplished and committed academic in the field of Biomedical Sciences and to ultimately pass on that knowledge through continued academic research and teaching.

Example 14

Studying Biomedical Science appeals to me as it is underpins so many of the advances in Biology and Medicine that have developed rapidly in recent years, such as nuclear medicine and genetic engineering. As I envisage being involved in further scientific research in the future, this degree will provide me with a broad base of relevant knowledge from which to progress to a specialism. After leaving school I took up a place at Medical School in my home country of Iraq and studied there for two years until a personal situation meant that I reluctantly had to leave. Now, as a mature student, I am fully appreciative of the opportunity to return to university and I am in a position to commit myself entirely to degree study.

My experience of and interest in studying Medical Science has motivated me to apply for Biomedical Science, as this was the area I found most fascinating. Studying scientific principles has allowed me to understand the basic processes governing the function of the body and I found practical experiments and hands-on work to be a particularly memorable way to learn. The more theoretical areas also motivate me and at university I look forward to broadening my knowledge of the life sciences. I am looking forward to further study of the diseases that affect the human body and their causes, treatment and prevention. In particular I hope to gain a deeper understanding of biochemistry, human biology, anatomy, radiology and nuclear medicine. Allied subjects such as data analysis using IT and the ethics of medical science also interest me, as they will be very useful for my future professional development. My two years' study in Medical School has ensured that I have experience of the requirements of degree level academic work. At my former university I maintained an excellent record of attendance and contribution to classes and I intend to bring the same level of commitment to studying in the UK.

My employment history has also given me skills and experience that will transfer well to life as a student. Working for the Iraqi civil service, within the Department of Social Security, required me to interact frequently with the public and with colleagues at different ranks within the department, giving me confident communication and interpersonal skills. My duties involved handling transactions between the Treasury and customers, and this has developed in me a professional and responsible manner. Having experienced working life and been exposed to a range of jobs and careers has also reinforced my commitment to obtain a degree in a subject of interest to me, as it has demonstrated the personal satisfaction and increased opportunities which are available to graduates.

In my spare time I enjoy playing snooker and learning about wildlife through television shows, books and journals. I also enjoy improving my computing and IT skills, and I have completed my European Computer Driving Licence. Travelling is another interest, and I enjoy learning about different places, cultures and languages. In the future I am hoping to progress to Postgraduate study and a research career in Biomedical Science or Human Anatomy. As a mature applicant, I have researched my options carefully and I am confident that this degree programme, and the opportunities it gives for practical work experience, will prepare me for working towards my career goal.

Business

Example 15

As a final year A level student, I am looking forward to developing specialist knowledge in a particular area by undertaking a degree in Business Administration. As well as gaining a more detailed understanding of business, I hope to continue to develop the practical skills that will help me in my intended career in international business management.

During my A levels I have covered a range of areas in Business, including accounting, economics, statistics and the application of IT in business. In particular I have enjoyed learning about the development of small businesses and the effects of operating within an international market. Focusing on marketing tourism in Morocco, I have enjoyed applying marketing theories to the real life examples from the tourism industry. During my degree I am looking forward to developing these interests and I feel the increased focus on specialist areas of the industry will equip me well for my future professional development.

Undertaking extensive work experience in the business sector has provided me with a context for understanding the practical implementation of the theories I have studied. A three-month internship last summer gave me an insight into the use of accounting techniques and the different transactions dealt with by a bank. This was followed by a two-month training internship in the production department of a bottling company. Here I was able to learn about the production line process and was given an overview of the marketing strategies used by the company to promote their products.

At college I have involved myself with voluntary work such as organising a campaign to collect unwanted books from students and donate them to charities and libraries. In this way I have been able to build on my organisational and time management skills, prioritising my extra-curricular responsibilities with my academic workload.

As a fluent speaker of English, French and Arabic I have enjoyed volunteering my linguistic skills to help students in learning basic French. I am also continuing to learn Spanish myself, and am at intermediate level. My part time work around the college, undertaking tasks such as helping to arrange award ceremonies and giving directions to new students, has helped me to develop strong interpersonal and communication skills. I have also been able to acquire a good basis of office administration skills and IT proficiency, which will be useful for a future career in any field. Studying and living in several different countries has further shaped my personality, giving me confidence in my ability to adapt to new situations and an outgoing attitude.

In the future I intend to gain a wide spectrum of employment experience in different areas of business, and in the long term envisage myself as a director or manager of a multinational company or bank. I believe that this degree will provide me with the knowledge and technical skills required to progress successfully in this direction and I intend to make the most of every opportunity available to me at university.

Example 16

The complex world of business impacts on every aspect of modern life from an individual's employment to the economic development of a country. In studying Business Management at degree level, I hope to enhance my knowledge of all aspects of the industry in order to equip myself for a career as an entrepreneur and business manager. Studying for a UK degree will increase my prospects globally and I intend to build on my employment experience by making use of the opportunity of work placements during my degree.

My work history has been useful in introducing me to office life and the basics of how a business operates. In my first role, as a clerk for my present employer, my duties included administrative tasks such as typing, filing and booking appointments. This helped to develop my organisational skills and taught me the importance of punctuality, reliability and co-operative teamwork to all sectors of business. As an efficient and capable member of the team I have been promoted to office assistant and now have responsibility for accompanying prospective clients on property viewings and arranging appropriate mortgages. This position has required strengths in IT and interpersonal communication, which I feel will be an asset during my university studies. Throughout my employment I have proved myself to be a hardworking individual who is always ready to learn new things and improve my skills, and I intend to bring the same level of commitment to my future degree.

At university I am looking forward to learning all aspects of how business management practices affect the success of a company. The real life applications of the subject and the opportunity to learn via both theory and case studies fascinate me, as does the opportunity to set my own experience of business into an academic context. As a future business person I am especially interested in learning practical skills such as managing human resources and in understanding the most appropriate management strategies for different scenarios. The chance to study the accounting and economic aspects of running a business and the different approaches required by the public, private and international sectors is a further attraction of these courses, as this will help to prepare me fully for the job market.

Having lived and attended school in different countries, I have acquired a flexible and adaptable approach to learning which I feel will serve me well as I start university, and I enjoy meeting and working with new people. My travels have also opened my eyes to different cultures and languages, developing in me a more mature outlook. In leisure time I enjoy widening my IT skills via the internet and following football, and at university I intend to develop new skills and hobbies through involvement in different clubs and societies. In the long term I hope to increase my experience by working in a range of managerial positions, before utilising my entrepreneurial skills to set up my own business.

As a mature applicant I have an understanding of the wider context of the world of business, and have had the opportunity to assess my personal development needs and research my career options thoroughly. I am highly motivated towards achieving my ambitions and I look forward to taking full advantage of the opportunities available to me at university.

Chemistry

Example 17

The particular attraction of Chemistry above any other subject is the unique opportunity it creates to play an active and vital role in many aspects of our existence here on Earth. Molecular mechanisms and what they can tell us about our world fascinate me and a university course represents an ideal opportunity to further pursue my main interest. I have always been interested in science; all my work experience and extra-curricular activities have been geared towards it in one way or another. It was only during my A level course that I realised I wanted to specialise in Chemistry; no other science truly combines pure science and practical application in such a way, and I cannot wait to begin further study.

I am, however, enjoying the breadth and depth of my A level studies and relish the freedom to work more independently. I have found that Sixth Form study offers great scope for reading around my subjects and free periods give me the opportunity to work on solutions to problems before asking for any support or advice from my tutors. This year I am particularly looking forward to my Chemistry coursework project, as it will allow me to choose my research topic. Currently I am leaning towards organic Chemistry, looking particularly at the nuclear processes and whether other ways of generating energy are possible within other materials. The personal motivation required for success at A level has made my whole course of study much more rewarding than at GCSE level, something I can see increasing even further at university.

I have grasped every opportunity to learn more about Chemistry. During Year 10 I took part in work shadowing in the Medicinal Chemistry department at a pharmaceutical company, working in the synthesis labs, learning about Analytical Chemistry and related departments. I have taken part in two extra-curricular Chemistry courses including a residential Chemistry course and later this year I will be attending a hands-on mass spectroscopy session. These wonderful experiences helped to finalise my decisions about a career path and allowed me to meet people who shared my own passion for Chemistry. This year I was awarded the Year 12 prize for my work in Chemistry lessons. I read the 'Chemistry Review' magazine, which has taught me how to directly relate my A level syllabus to everyday situations. I enjoy reading popular science books; the most recent was 'The End of Time' by Julian Barbour. I also read works of fiction by authors such as Jane Austen and Graham Greene.

I have taken part in all three levels of the Duke of Edinburgh Award, and have been a Managing Director within the Young Enterprise scheme. I also spent time as the Student Council secretary. All of these experiences built my teamwork, managerial skills and developed my organisation skills. I managed to use the skills I learnt through the Duke of Edinburgh Award scheme by volunteering to be a team leader on a Year 7 Outward Bound course. I am an active person, having played lacrosse for my school team for four years, leading us to a gold medal in the National Schools' Lacrosse Championships last year.

I look forward to contributing fully to university life through music, sport, and study. I am certain my chosen course is right for me and am eager to take this opportunity to prove myself and to take the first step onto the ladder towards a fulfilling career in Chemistry.

Example 18

The challenge of understanding Chemistry and the issues that surround it as a subject are just two reasons why Chemistry appeals to me so much. Chemistry is so applicable to society; the ever-changing needs of our world today, especially in terms of Environmental Chemistry and Medicine, mean that Chemistry will always be relevant and essential no matter what career avenue I choose to pursue. A career in pharmaceuticals, research, management and the chemical manufacturing industry are all possible uses for a good Chemistry degree, and I intend to apply myself well to my studies to ensure that is what I achieve.

Much thought went into my decision to study Chemistry; I first had the idea because it is one of my favourite subjects. Then at a higher education fair, I went to a lecture entitled 'Why Chemistry?' which illustrated the lucrative and exciting career prospects. I attended general open days for science subjects; I greatly enjoyed visiting Chemistry departments, often chatting informally with undergraduates, increasing my thirst for the subject. I was able to gain more of an insight into the specialised nature of studying Chemistry to degree level, and understood better the research opportunities involved as well as the balance Chemistry provides of pure and applied science. I particularly enjoy practical experimentation and so was pleased to discover that it forms a large part of the degree programme.

I have recently completed work shadowing at a laboratory, where I learnt how a modern analytical industrial chemistry laboratory functions. I am a regular reader of both the 'Chemistry Review' and 'Chemistry in Britain'. Additionally, I am currently the only member of both staff and student groups at our school, as I work as a laboratory technician repairing and constructing laboratory apparatus as required by heads of subject. My work mainly involves Physics, though the improvisational scientific techniques that I have learnt have improved my general experimental ability.

I lead an active and varied social life, but by far my main extra-curricular pursuit has to be diving. I have been diving for six years and have recently been eligible to compete at the Manchester Watersports Association Games representing the South West in three separate diving events. This year at the MWA Games I achieved two Gold placings and a Bronze, and I am determined to continue diving at university, though not to the detriment of my studies. I also enjoy helping with amateur dramatics, assisting by setting up and running special effects, lighting and sound. I am often responsible for the organisational process, which is very time consuming but satisfying. I have done this for a total of 16 operas, plays, musicals, and pantomimes with five different organisations. I also helped take the school opera on tour to the Czech Republic as the only member of the lighting and sound crew.

I am a well-rounded, level-headed and developed student with a mature work ethic and an excellent attendance and punctuality record. I am committed to both a degree course and a career in the field of Chemistry, and see university as only the first step on the ladder of both academic and life learning.

Classical Studies

Example 19

As an A level History student, one of the first things I learnt about History is that there is never just one simple answer as to why certain events have taken place in the past. As a result of studying History at A level I have been able to develop skills of analysis, researching and selecting appropriate material. I have also been able to critically evaluate primary and secondary sources, which has provided me with the ability to form my own coherent judgments and opinions on historical events. I have always enjoyed studying all of the Humanities, but the study of History and the Classics has remained my most dominant interest. My thirst for knowledge of the past began at an early age; school and family trips to historical sites such as the Tower of London, Canterbury and Stonehenge as a child were emotionally stimulating and deepened my appreciation for learning about times past.

I have found the modules I have studied in History extremely interesting. In particular, I found studying the Greek philosophy an enlightening topic, which gave me insight into how reflective thinking can have such an impact on the development of a culture. I also found it amazing how the Greek and Roman civilisations have played such a significant role in shaping the society of today. From studying the Roman legacy my views on the world changed significantly. I also found studying the various Roman Emperors interesting; what was fascinating was that through very different approaches to ruling the Roman Empire, these heads of state were able to grow and expand the Empire to achieve global domination.

As a result of my interests in History and the Classics I would like to further expand my studies and gain a much wider knowledge of the past. This particular course means that I will be given the chance to spread my studies across ancient and more recent worlds and combine History with Classics. Studying in London is also tremendously important to me; London is a city full of history, and as a History student I would have the positive opportunity to draw on the resources of a city which is the United Kingdom's centre of government, law, commerce, finance and culture.

While at school I was able to take on the role of Form Prefect, showing responsibility, dedication and a sense of duty towards school life and my fellow students. I co-ordinated a Netball club and was part of the Science Club, and during Sixth Form I was part of a team that led younger students through their Bronze Duke of Edinburgh Award expedition. I have also been involved in charity work for Save The Children.

During my AS levels I had a part-time job working for a department store; my duties included cash handling, customer liaisons, and various other duties. It was while working there that I realised the importance of working as part of a team. During busy seasonal periods I was under great pressure to respond quickly to customer demands, yet due to the co-operation of colleges and good teamwork, potential problems were avoided and customers were left satisfied.

I am determined and highly motivated, especially when studying subjects I enjoy. I strongly believe that being able to study History and Classics will give me the opportunity to develop a higher level of analytical skills and knowledge, meaning I will be able to form a much more accurate opinion on events which have taken place in the past, which is essential as a Historian.

Example 20

Through my work at a local museum, by helping voluntarily at History Club and through an extensive catalogue of extra-curricular reading, my most important aim for the next few years is to further my knowledge of Classical Studies in every way possible. History is by no means a subject that is past its sell by date; it is very much alive in almost every aspect of our modern society, and through studying the subject at GCSE and A level I have extended my interest in Social, European and Classical History, and how this relates to World History.

As a student of History, I aim to extend my analytical and presentational skills. Once given an area to study, I like to research independently, but I am also able to work well with others. My time at Sixth Form College has enabled me to improve my reliability, punctuality and ability to work independently, while coping with the demands of exams and deadlines. I believe my AS levels complement each other particularly well, enabling me to use the knowledge of one subject to develop my understanding of another. They have also extended my abilities in research and essay and report writing. My AS results proved pleasing and, after analysing my results, have enabled me to set realistic targets for the year ahead.

In addition to my academic studies I have achieved qualifications in First Aid, and I feel confident to administer help in unlikely situations. Over the past two years, I have helped with a play scheme connected with my County Council in which I had responsibility for looking after and helping children. In my spare time, I enjoy reading non-fiction books, and travelling to see many parts of the country. My Duke of Edinburgh Award scheme enabled me to deal effectively with decision making within a group, and this year I was proud to receive my Gold Award from the Duke himself.

Out of College, I have had a part-time job at a newsagent for just over two years. This role has given me responsibilities such as dealing with customers, taking stock and dealing with large amounts of money, which meant I had to be organised and punctual at all times. At my secondary school, I helped to set up a School Council as I felt that there were student issues that needed to be dealt with. Work experience at an Estate Agent in Cambridge gave me good experience of working in a city and commuting, and also insight into an area of business. In my impending Gap Year, I intend to travel and work at an orphanage near to Jakarta, which I have maintained links with since a trip in Sixth Form, and also to New Zealand. I am confident that my future career in the field of History and Classical Studies lies abroad, possibly within teaching or research.

My main priority for now is to complete my A levels to the best of my ability and to go on to university, not just for the degree but for the entire experience it has to offer and I look forward to moving on, learning and meeting new people.

Computing

Example 21

Having studied the technical and practical aspects of Computer Science for several years via the Association of Computer Professionals (ACP) programme, I now wish to make up my Advanced Diploma to a BSc through direct entry into the 3rd Year. For several years I have combined my studies with a full time career, but I am now in a position to commit myself fully to a year of university study in order to gain a respected qualification and launch my career as an IT specialist.

Through the ACP I have gained a thorough understanding of computer theory, software engineering, business information systems, computing architecture, networking and computer management. I am proficient with several programming languages, including QBasic, Visual Basic Pascal and Java, and have completed projects based on real systems in each language. I have particularly enjoyed learning the practical aspects of programming and studying modules designed to help us become more effective IT practitioners in the future. For my Advanced Diploma final project I have appreciated the opportunity to concentrate on one topic, focussing on Structured System Analysis and Design Methodology. I have now set myself the target of achieving my Bachelor's degree in the next academic year and I am committed to making the most of the short time I will spend at university. In particular I look forward to studying Business alongside advancing my knowledge of computing, as I believe the two subjects will be closely related throughout my future career.

Originally starting a job as a cashier in December 2006, I have progressed to the managerial position of Customer and Trading Support, learning a great deal about business operations along the way. My employment history has also given me varied experience of working within a team environment, and more recently of supporting and motivating a team and of interacting with colleagues from all backgrounds and at all levels. Working in customer facing roles has developed in me confident communication and interpersonal skills as I deal with complaints and potentially difficult customers on a daily basis. My contribution to the management of a large company has also motivated my interest in studying Business at university, and I am looking forward to learning about some of the theories I have seen used in practice.

Outside of my work I attend and participate in a theocratic school at which I have learnt to communicate articulately and with confidence, making use of gestures, facial expressions and vocal tone to improve my delivery. At university I hope to implement the skills I have learnt here during presentations and when in academic discussions with fellow students. In my leisure time I enjoy playing football and following sports such as tennis and basketball. I particularly relish opportunities for debates on topical issues and I intend to continue to develop these interests through club involvement at university. In the future I envisage myself working in a computing environment in which I can interact both with professionals such as programmers and analysts, and with business and domestic customers. I am confident that I have the skills and motivation to succeed at university and that this is the appropriate next step towards me achieving my goal of becoming an IT professional.

Example 22

The computer world is expanding rapidly and I feel that nowadays, more than ever before, it is important to keep up with the new technological advances as these are the future. Over the years my interest in the world of computer technology has grown from small home computers to the Internet, and I have decided that I would eventually like a career in this field. A university degree would enable me to succeed to the best of my ability.

The Internet has fascinated me for sometime now, from web page design to computer security. The idea that any information is easily and rapidly accessible from any connected computer terminal in the world is fascinating; indeed, computer technology has always been something that I have been intrigued by, from my very first Atari to the small home network that I now manage. I am extremely fortunate to be studying Information Technology in a specialised Technology College, which has national recognition, as it is also a Beacon School and the only Learning Network Community with radio WAN equipment in the region. I have taken advantage of these excellent facilities in my role as Student Software and IT Manager; I am responsible for making sure all students have access to such facilities by supervising computer rooms and instructing younger students as to how to use the equipment correctly.

In 2000, I undertook work experience in two business venues in Liverpool, these being the offices of a taxi firm and a family run guest house. I used the computer systems for tasks such as booking customers' rooms at the hotel and editing taxi drivers' records. Although the work that I did on the computers was very basic and did not specifically concern the Internet or programming, I feel that it has helped me to recognise how even the smallest departments of the business world rely on computers for everyday tasks.

I have also gained experience with computers through the Young Enterprise programme, during which I was

IT Director of our company. I designed, managed and maintained the company website, which included processing online customer orders. This helped me to realise the responsibility of meeting deadlines, as when deadlines were not met the whole company was let down and not just the individual. During this marketing experience we visited primary schools, where I gave a PowerPoint presentation to promote our product. The products produced were contemporary photo frames made from recycled materials. Our company enjoyed much success; winning a trip to the European Trade Fair in Brussels, being featured on many occasions in the media and winning through to the North West Final. At this final, although we did not win outright, we did win an award for best customer service - largely due to the accessibility of our website! This experience has improved my confidence greatly, as well as giving me an insight into the world of marketing and promotion. Being in three school plays has also added to my confidence, as I find that now I am more prepared for public speaking.

As I look forward to my dreams, I see myself as a confident, successful businesswoman with a university degree and a computer related career. I know that studying at your institution will make my dream a reality, and I cannot wait to start.

Criminology

Example 23

My interest in concepts of criminality, human rights and social justice stems primarily from having lived in many different countries, with very varied standards of living, and having had the opportunity to compare attitudes to these issues across different cultures and religions. This has been supplemented by regularly reading journals and magazines such as New Internationalist, Justice and Geographical, as well as newspaper articles covering similar topics. Studying Critical Criminology at university will allow me to develop this interest to a much higher level and prepare me for further research.

Studying Geography at A level has provided an academic background to my love of travelling and I have been fascinated to learn about the social, cultural and economic situations of different areas of the world. My coursework on the issue of local regeneration has opened my eyes to some of the social problems faced by British cities, including the use of town planning techniques to reduce crime. English Literature has allowed me to explore the views and perspectives of people in different socio-economic groups, and the ways in which they express them. At university I would like to continue these themes by taking modules focusing on the role of the media in disseminating information about crime and in influencing popular opinion, social policy and legal changes regarding crime. Widening the issue of criminality to include state violence and war will be very interesting, as it expands the boundaries of who we consider to be a criminal and whether criminal behaviour is ever acceptable. At college I have enjoyed every opportunity to conduct my own research, following my own interests and ideas, and I am very excited about acquiring skills in social science research and utilising these during my essays and dissertation.

Having participated in the National Youth Theatre for the last five years, I regularly take part in Speech and Drama festivals across Yorkshire and have won first prize in several regional Public Speaking contests. This has helped me develop confidence in effective verbal communication in front of a big audience. My travelling experiences have also improved my self-reliance and independence and given me confidence in my ability to adapt to unfamiliar situations. I am a keen sportswoman and play football, rugby, hockey, cricket and tennis at competition level. My achievements include winning regional and international tournaments in club football and representing Yorkshire Under-17s in hockey. I play cricket for the school first team as well as for a local club. In athletics I have been ranked highly in national youth championships for 100 metre sprints and triple jump. My sports have taught me the skills of teamwork, communication, discipline and commitment essential for a successful career in any field. I also have an interest in music, playing 2nd violin in the string orchestra at concerts.

In the future I hope to stay at university and undertake further research into areas of Criminology. My varied interests provide me with a healthy balance to my academic achievements and I am looking forward to making a positive contribution to both the extra-curricular and academic life of the university.

Example 24

In pursuing a Criminology degree I look forward to analysing the precedents and controversies which have contributed to our legal system and shaped our society. Researching the subject and discussing it whilst on work experience I have been fascinated by the extent to which the legal system affects every aspect of the functioning of a country. This degree will provide me with an academic challenge and I feel I will benefit from developing my capacity for problem solving and critical analysis.

At school I have felt the benefit of the freedom to develop my own study patterns and pursue my academic interests during S6. Close analysis and interpretation of texts has been an enjoyable aspect of both English and History A level, developing my appreciation of the power of words. History has also provided me with the context through which to learn about the development of the legal and judicial system. I have particularly enjoyed the opportunity to participate in school debates such as a recent one on the changes to Scottish licensing laws, which have given me confidence in presenting and justifying my research and ideas. At university I look forward to studying Policing and Criminal Law.

Working at a Citizens' Advice Bureau has given me an insight into the intrinsic importance of the law in all aspects of society's functioning. In particular I gained an appreciation of how powerless some people are, such as a homeless man whose interview I observed. This has opened my eyes to the need to ensure equality of access to the law and courts for all. I spent my work experience at a local Police station and was amazed by the sheer breadth and enormity of cases that local police have to deal with. I was particularly intrigued by the crimes which young people were involved in and would like to learn more about this.

On the Entertainments Committee at school I work within a team of pupils to organise social events such as discos, increasing my organisational and interpersonal skills. I also assist younger children with learning difficulties, providing a positive role model, particularly for those with dyslexia. In leisure time I play rugby on the local and school 1st XV teams, as well as hill running and canoeing. I have played lead roles with solos in several recent musicals, and with my band I recently won first prize in the school talent show. An expedition last year, canoeing down the Soper River in Canada, was an unforgettable experience. Through car boot sales I raised sufficient money, and then spent time preparing for the extreme physical and mental challenges. The conditions were harsh but in completing the trip, which included meeting Inuits, I witnessed an alternative, minimalist and materially poor lifestyle which has enlightened me in respect of the many global injustices.

After graduation I intend to become a youth worker, specialising in youth crime and working to allow equal legal representation for all who need it. As a highly motivated student with a variety of interests I feel that I have the qualities and motivation required to succeed in both my degree and my future career.

Dentistry

Example 25

Throughout my school years I have sought a challenging and rewarding profession that would satisfy my passion for science and the need to express my artistic and dextrous abilities, whilst allowing me to work closely with people to make a positive impact in their lives. Frequent visits to the dentist for orthodontic treatment triggered my fascination with dentistry and fuelled my aspirations to pursue a career in this demanding yet satisfying profession. I have a strong desire to not only improve the health and wellbeing of people, but to embark on a

life-long experience of learning and development in which I can constantly improve my knowledge and practical skills and embrace technological advancements in clinical dentistry.

My work experience at four dental practices has further reinforced my determination to study Dentistry. I was privileged to be able to shadow and assist dental practitioners; carrying out suction on patients undergoing procedures, sterilising instruments and developing x-rays. While I observed an Orthodontist, a Periodontist and an Oral Surgeon as they performed procedures such as fillings, root canal treatments, extractions, implants, flap surgery and the fitting of braces, I was struck by the immense patience, attention to detail and precision with which this intricate work was carried out. I learnt too, the importance of responsive communication with the patients and derived great satisfaction from being able to reassure and calm nervous patients before and during their treatment. My work as a dental receptionist during the summer months expanded my interpersonal, management and teamwork skills and gave me a valuable insight into the effective functioning of a busy dental practice. Teamwork is an important part of my voluntary and charity activities as well, particularly my involvement with Saint Francis Hospice where staff, volunteers, and families work together to ensure the best quality of life for terminally ill patients.

Having travelled to India and witnessing poverty and hardship I feel strongly that I want to continue to help others wherever possible. I am a member of a volunteer team at a school for children with special needs, where I enjoy taking responsibility for mentoring children, helping them to achieve their goals, providing support and responding to their individual needs. I plan to expand my volunteer work in my gap year by taking part in teaching projects in India and Nepal.

As a sociable and practical person, I found the responsibility of running clubs and activities at school immensely rewarding. Sewing and embroidery is a long standing hobby so I organised a school textiles club in which I could develop my manual dexterity and teach other members to create intricate patchwork and embroidered pieces. My passion for science and maths inspired me to run a science club and an economics club in which I could mentor younger students in areas in which they were struggling, and get involved in lively debates concerning current controversial issues. Being a member of the school magazine was a great opportunity to expand my organisational and teamwork skills to regularly produce interesting and informative articles against a strict deadline.

I am a committed, determined and hardworking person looking forward to the responsibility and challenges of studying at university. I am confident I will be able to balance the academic demands of the course with social and relaxing activities such as badminton and yoga, and will be organised and enthusiastic in my approach to my studies. I am fully aware of the lengthy and demanding nature of the course but my commitment and motivation convinces me I will achieve my ambition and make a positive contribution to the field of dentistry.

Example 26

My decision to study Dentistry at university is the result of careful consideration and it has required much determination on my part. With a view to studying Dentistry at university, and in order to reinforce the strength of my application, I have gained a number of further qualifications, the most significant of which is a Bachelors of Science. I particularly enjoyed performing dissections on a variety of organisms including frogs and earthworms. These regular practices required manual dexterity to ensure that these procedures were performed carefully and accurately. My enjoyment of this course, and in particular those areas which covered the human body, has confirmed my decision to study Dentistry.

Participating in work experience at a dental surgery has given me an invaluable insight into the day-to-day life of a dentist, and it has fuelled my desire to become one. During my experience, I observed many procedures including root canals, fillings and teeth removal. I learnt how to a take a patient's history and along with this, how to empathise with patients in situations that they may find stressful. I plan to build on this work experience with another upcoming placement, something which I have organised myself as a result of my eagerness to learn. Maxillofacial surgery is something that I am particularly eager to study in greater depth, and it could perhaps offer an area of specialism to me.

Being voted Head Girl in 2008 was a rewarding but challenging experience. It required me to act as a point of communication between my fellow pupils and teachers, and I was also responsible for the organisation of various events; one such event being a fun fair. I also had to ensure that the school rules were adhered to; this required excellent interpersonal skills in order to communicate my point to my fellow pupils. As Head of the Drama Society at school my responsibilities included organising the overall management of productions as well as casting and directing. This required excellent communication skills in order to get the best results from the actors. These skills can only be an asset as a dentist, as it is important to communicate effectively with patients. It also necessitated good organisational skills: I had to consider all aspects of the production, from arranging rehearsal times to sourcing props. I was also a member of the school debating team and competed in many inter-school competitions. My best performance saw me achieve second place in a regional final and this debating experience has improved my confidence and public speaking skills. My involvement with the Drama Society and debating team was a thoroughly enjoyable experience and they are something I would hope to continue with at university.

In my spare time I enjoy playing badminton, and I intend to continue this and make full use of the sporting facilities that university can offer me. At school I was a keen member of the cricket team and the netball team. My participation in these sports was invaluable in that it has helped me to learn how to work successfully in a team, and it allowed me to make many new friends. I also enjoy glass painting. This has allowed me to develop my artistic ability and also my manual dexterity, something that is essential in dentistry.

While my route to dentistry may not be as conventional as many others, I would hope that my determination and commitment to my future career are unquestionable. This course can help me to fulfil my future career ambitions whilst, in the process, allowing me to fully develop as a person.

Ecology

Example 27

My motivation to study Ecology comes from a desire to gain the scientific knowledge and practical skills necessary to eventually contribute to the scientific literature of this fascinating, multidisciplinary subject. I have undertaken weekly voluntary work which involves habitat maintenance and management work throughout the year. Among the many activities I have been involved in are hedge laying, coppicing and fence construction and ecological surveys and monitoring. This experience has taught me a great deal about the ecology of my local area, improved my teamwork and communication skills, and equipped me with the practical skills and subject knowledge I will require as an undergraduate studying Ecology.

I am particularly looking forward to studying modules in 'Ecotourism', 'African Wildlife', 'Biology and Game Parks' and 'Humans and Wildlife'. Ecotourism is an especially fascinating subject because, despite the avowed intention to be environmentally sensitive, it is often the case that ecotourism can cause problems to very sensitive habitats and environments. My interest in the relationship between humans and wildlife stems from the fact that we, as a species, have become estranged from our natural surroundings and this issue was recently brought home to me after watching film maker Werner Herzog's documentary 'Grizzly Man'.

This summer, I took part in an expedition to Tanzania to organise local community projects. It was both challenging and rewarding, and a fascinating insight into the markedly different habitats of a country on a different continent. The trip broadened my cultural horizons and required me to respect local customs and act with sensitivity. I was also able to teach English to a class of 50 children, a very daunting experience but one which I relished. I also fulfilled a personal ambition by climbing Mount Meru and overcoming my fear of heights. Experiencing new cultures is something that I particularly enjoy, hence my continuing with Italian lessons at school to improve my language skills.

Representing my school in rowing has been an enjoyable experience, although it required much dedication. Our ability as a team was demonstrated when, as an Under-16s Team, we beat a university women's team in a regatta. Drama provides an outlet for my creativity and has given me greater confidence in public speaking. This is something that I intend to continue at university. I also take great pleasure in horse riding and I compete my own horses in affiliated dressage and cross-country competitions, where I have achieved success including qualifying for summer and winter regional finals in dressage.

In conclusion, the variety of my experiences relating to ecology and habitat management has reinforced my desire to follow a career in a sub-field of Ecology and I hope they demonstrate I have the motivation and conscientious attitude needed to succeed. The breadth of my extra-curricular activities indicates not only the ways in which I can contribute to university life, but also demonstrates that I have a well balanced approach to my studies. This surely will be an asset when it comes to coping with the pressures that studying Ecology will inevitably entail.

Example 28

My motivation to study Ecology stems from my passion for understanding how organisms interact within ecosystems, and the complex and varied processes which this entails. As a child I took an immense interest in the natural world around me, and I spent a great deal of time reading about the flora and fauna native to Britain and attempting to identify everything I encountered on family walks in the countryside. In school I have been fascinated to explore the functions of a range of plants and animals in Biology, while Chemistry has stimulated my curiosity into the mechanisms by which these processes are governed. In my degree I am particularly looking forward to taking a holistic approach to the subject and learning more about the flow of energy through an ecosystem, and the effects and implications of climate change. As I enjoy practical manual work, I am also excited by the prospect of field trips.

My involvement with a nature association has given invaluable insights into the ecology of the British Isles and, as a branch member, I have taken part in talks and exploratory wildlife walks across Britain under the guidance of knowledgeable and expert naturalists. Being a committee member of these societies I have organised talks and prepared flyers which has developed my skills in written and verbal communication. As a mentor for Year 9 students I take pride in advising and supporting younger pupils through their GCSE choices. I am also a Prefect, assisting staff with the smooth running of the school. Organising a Christmas show for the elderly, I learnt the value of cohesive teamwork as we made group decisions about the content and delivery of entertainment and catering. Having already achieved my Bronze and Silver, I am now working towards my Gold Duke of Edinburgh Award, and have already completed the six-day expedition. This required our team to work closely over a sustained period, planning the expedition for months beforehand and supporting each other during the trip. For four years I have had a daily paper round and am now the Team Leader, organising the papers for delivery for four others, developing my confidence and leadership.

Through work placements I have gained a great deal of experience of scientific work in the field, as well as the opportunity to spend time in a scientific library learning about the process of information gathering and how scientific results are published as reports and papers in scientific journals. Through this experience I gained an appreciation of both the practical and academic skills which a degree in Ecology will entail. This experience has affirmed my conviction to study a degree in Ecology and pursue a career within the field of climatology.

At school I have maintained an effective balance of academic work, responsibilities and other activities. I am on the school hockey team, and also play golf, football and table tennis. Constructing working radio-controlled models, such as cars and helicopters, fulfils my passion for understanding how things work. Writing poetry gives me another creative outlet, and I recently won an inter-house poetry competition. I also enjoy reading about ecological issues, focusing on understanding how organisms and non-organic processes interact to affect changes in habitat and climate.

In the long term I hope to make use of my expertise by working in the field of climatology. I am a highly motivated and hard working student, dedicated to working in this field, and I feel I have the qualities and commitment required for success at university and in my future career.

Economics

Example 29

Since studying Politics and Economics at A level I have found these to be engaging and stimulating subjects, with significant relevance to the contemporary world. In studying a degree in this area I hope to enhance my understanding of the social, economic and governmental structures through which a country is run and to develop the skills to critically analyse and evaluate the varied approaches used by different countries around the world. My intention is to pursue a career in the field of international economics and I am confident that this degree programme will give me ample opportunity to acquire the knowledge and expertise required for this job market.

During my A level study I have enjoyed learning about the interdependence of many aspects of Politics and Economics, and through this combined approach I have come to understand the principles behind managing a country's economy, developing its political stability and anticipating the future consequences of any political or economic changes. The potentially far-reaching nature of these changes particularly fascinates me, as in a global market economy any individual may be directly affected by the actions of another individual on a different continent. I am also attracted to the requirement of keeping permanently up-to-date with developments in political and economic systems, as well as in academic theories. In order to maintain my ability to contribute a valid argument to debates, I regularly read the Economist and the daily broadsheets. As a Maths student I also enjoy the numerical aspect of macroeconomics, and have been fascinated to learn about the influence fiscal and monetary policies can have on a country's economy. At university, I am particularly keen to further my knowledge and understanding of macroeconomics, the social contract and all aspects of politics.

In addition to my A levels, my attendance at a summer school in 2007, at which I achieved Honours in Social

Ethics, American Foreign Policy and Speech Making, has significantly widened my understanding of these subjects. Studying the social contract and the reasons why individuals feel the need to form a society and why societies need governments, law and justice, was particularly enlightening. I also welcomed the chance to study the views of theorists such as Socrates on society's laws, and to discuss and debate these issues with fellow students from a range of experiences. This extra study, and the attendant opportunity to develop my communication and interpersonal skills, was well utilised during my two-week internship at Nuon, a leading energy company. This gave me first hand experience of the principles of supply and demand, the effects of fluctuations in the pricing of natural resources, and the use of market hedges premiums to compensate for this uncertainty. In the credit risk department, I also learned how a large company quantifies and manages financial risk. This placement was complemented by a week's internship at an international law firm, where I assisted a senior associate with issues such as netting and tolling agreements between energy companies.

At school I have developed leadership skills through my roles as Prefect and Sixth Form Committee Member, and I intend to contribute similarly to the university community. In the long term I hope to combine my passions for politics and economics through a career with a major institution such as the World Bank or the United Nations. I consider myself a confident and well-motivated student and I look forward to the challenges and rewards of life and study at university.

Example 30

My interest in business and economic affairs began prior to 1997 when I became aware of the enormous economic changes in Hong Kong. The crucial role that economics plays in national and international trade has motivated me to apply for these degree programmes. By extensive reading and subscribing to The Economist and The Times, I have widened my exposure to world business and economic affairs. This has reinforced my future goals and persuaded me that taking AS Economics in my final year will enable me to appreciate market forces in greater detail and prepare me further for my degree. At university, I am excited about studying Economics, Business Management, Globalisation and Development Studies. I speak fluent Cantonese and the traditional Chinese dialect, Hakka, and I anticipate spending some time working in Hong Kong, either during my gap year or after graduating prior to taking up a permanent position in the United Kingdom.

My choice of A level subjects reflects my creative nature. Maths challenges me, whilst Graphics and Photography allow me to demonstrate my ability to collect and collate information, organise data and meet deadlines. This has provided me with excellent IT skills which will be of great help when preparing assignments and presentations at university. As a school prefect I have improved my interpersonal skills, carrying out my duties diligently and acting as a role model for younger children. Being recognised for outstanding achievements in 2005, I was proud to represent my school at a Commonwealth ceremony held at Westminster Abbey in front of the Queen. This proved a major motivator towards succeeding in my exams and future studies.

During my two-week work experience in retailing, I observed the competitive nature of marketing as my time coincided with an intensive sales promotion at a particular target audience. I was introduced to working under pressure and adopting a flexible approach. As a finance and market research administrative assistant I enhanced my communication and organisational skills, whilst working as a waitress has shown me the importance of teamworking and good customer relations. As a first aid assistant, I have completed a First Aid at Work course and attend functions for over 500 people. This has heightened my sense of responsibility as I assist those injured and provide reassurance and support in addition to reporting incidents accurately. To further increase my commercial knowledge, I have a pending application for work experience at the Bank of New York.

In October 2004, I volunteered as a co-ordinator for the 'Min Quan & Broomfield' event to raise money for the Morecambe Bay campaign. This was challenging as it required strong interpersonal skills. In my spare time, I enjoy paintballing, art and design, and reading. My hobby is painting, which relaxes me, and I attend church and regularly participate in the Young Fellowship service and group. This, combined with all of the above, will help me to succeed in my course and provide an outlet to the inevitable pressures of university by providing a balance to my studies. My ambition is to work as an economist in the UK after studying for a Masters degree. As an enthusiastic and committed individual, I look forward to university and am confident that my academic success and work experience will stand me in good stead.

Engineering

Example 31

Technology is advancing at a rapid rate and one of my greatest ambitions is to aid this growth and make a difference. Daily life has been revolutionised over the past generation by the development of electronics and I would value a career in a fast changing environment that thrives on performance and innovation. The challenges of analysis and problem solving that engineering provides are of great interest to me and in pursuing this degree I seek to advance my knowledge of electrical systems, particularly in the growing field of nanotechnology, which I ultimately plan to embrace. I am enthusiastic about the sandwich option, aiming to secure sponsorship with a local company, as this will provide me with practical experience of industrial work.

My choice of science related A levels established the strong academic foundation necessary for success; excelling as an international candidate with fluent English. My success in Further Mathematics has stimulated me to begin a career in a closely related field, while studying Physics both individually and as part of a team has been an inspiring experience. A vital reason for studying Engineering in the UK is the access to sophisticated equipment to investigate more advanced level Physics. Additionally I am also looking forward to the impressive Student Union not yet present in my home country.

It is my belief that success as an engineer nowadays requires technical competence and a combination of management, leadership, communication and business skills. My leadership and communication skills improved working full-time in my country this summer. The main aim of this was to provide an insight into the world of work and the demands that are made upon a worker on a daily basis. Therefore, after deciding to become an engineer, I set out to find the qualities necessary for success. In the process, I read about Thomas Edison, Isambard Brunel, and a host of others, finally reaching an answer that it is helpful to succeed both as a talented engineer and as a brilliant business person.

I have varied interests, with football serving as a particularly rewarding hobby. I have played football for my county from 2005-2008, but I have left it now as my studies are my main priority. I take an active interest in other sports too and have regularly participated in

inter-house matches in cricket, tennis and football which I will continue at university. Currently, I am learning the piano, which I believe will help me thrive mentally and aid relaxation. In addition, I have nurtured a long standing interest in computing and the internet, as well as both communications and media. As a side activity after my A levels, I taught myself various forms of BASIC to Object-Oriented languages, which will be valuable in Electrical Engineering. Lately, I have been learning French, and I hope to continue my practice of taking different language classes alongside my university studies. My desire to learn new languages is always present and I am fluent in Hindi, Urdu, Arabic, and Bengali. Visiting new places enables me to mix with people from different cultural backgrounds and this has given me added maturity.

Having been brought up with strong family values, I have been taught the importance of further education. I have the character and strength of personality to make a success of it and by participating fully in university life I hope to reach my full potential. I believe a degree in Engineering will be the first step toward my long-term ambition to found an engineering consulting firm in my home country.

Example 32

Over recent years the present generation has witnessed a revolution in wireless communication that has touched almost all areas of life, whether in the commercial workplace, in education, healthcare or in the home. This rapid advancement of wireless technology opens up an exciting future for electronic and communications engineers and one which I am keen to pursue. I would love to follow a career within this fast changing environment where I would have the opportunity to be innovative by exploiting new materials and technologies, adapt to the changing markets and to constantly explore new ideas.

Having excelled in Mathematics at school I went on to work within Telecommunications and I found that this area fascinated me, particularly the study of wireless communications. I became very interested in the way in which mobile phones have evolved over a relatively short space of time so that they now utilise wireless networks and Bluetooth technologies. After I completed an evening course in wireless communication I knew that I had an enquiring mind and I very much wanted to commit to an area that fascinated me such as computer security, ad hoc wireless networks or sensor networks. My experience of the workplace has taught me to apply a disciplined and thoughtful approach to the way in which I carry out my work and I enjoy making a positive contribution. My work ethos is one of hard-work and organisation, with the ability to work on my own independently when necessary. After five years of working, I now feel as though I would like to further develop my knowledge by undertaking a degree in Engineering. As a student I am particularly looking forward to discussing my areas of interest with my peers and sharing ideas and experiences in network forums with other students and tutors. My time as Union Representative at work has taught me to rise to the challenge of being responsible for putting across the views of others and I would welcome the opportunity to take on similar responsibilities at university.

I look forward to being able to study at your institution, not only because of the high standard of teaching, combined with the internationally recognised research profile in the area of Electronic Engineering, but also because it would give me the opportunity to expand my cultural horizons and experiences. As well as socialising, my interests include playing badminton, classical music (I enjoy attending classical concerts and playing the piano), travel and fine cuisine. I am keen to meet new people and to get involved in the various activities and clubs that university has to offer. I believe it is important to balance the pressures of hard work associated with academic study with relaxation, physical activity and social interaction.

I am convinced that my decision to study for a degree in Electrical Engineering and Computer Science is the right one and, although I know the work will be demanding, I am confident that my motivation to succeed and my hard-working nature will ensure I will achieve my goal of becoming an accomplished researcher and teacher in my chosen field of wireless communications.

English

Example 33

Through GCSE and A level literature courses, I have been able to refine an ongoing and developing interest in English Literature and the science of Linguistics into a focused, analytical appreciation of all areas of English study. I am particularly fascinated by the way literature has both influenced and been influenced by the history and culture of society. For this very reason, I especially enjoy 20th century prose, including the novels of E.M. Forster; literature often serves the purpose of immortalising history whilst mixing it so beautifully with fantasy.

My diverse range of A level options means that I have been able to adopt a mature and balanced attitude to many issues and topics, often discovering links between my chosen subjects. Studying German has allowed me an insight into a different culture, whilst also reinforcing the rules and structures of many areas of linguistics. I chose Physics as a contrasting subject to English and German because of the different demands and disciplines included within the subject and the way it requires logical and structured thought. This balanced approach to problems will be useful both at university and in my future career.

My career plans are still open at this stage, but I do have a certain interest in the world of publishing. I would enjoy the challenge of analysing and predicting the desires of readers, particularly in an age where IT and the Internet have changed many people's attitudes to books. To gain experience of the publishing industry I have started volunteer work in a charity bookshop dealing specifically with out-of-print, rare volumes. Often I have to deal with publishers on a one-to-one basis, allowing me a unique insight into the publishing world from the point of view of both a retailer and an avid reader.

I am equipping myself for future study and employment by accepting positions of responsibility both in and outside school. Within school I am Head Prefect, meaning that

I work closely with my peers, teachers and younger pupils. This position has developed my organisational and communication skills. I have also worked for the past year as a literacy monitor and 'reading friend'. This has meant assisting in the school's campaign to raise literacy standards and also helping younger pupils to improve their reading. As well as the satisfaction of seeing improved standards and the fun of sharing books with others, I have been able to gain teaching experience and a better understanding of language issues and problems.

Outside school, I have a long-standing commitment to voluntary work. For several years I have held the position of Head Cadet in my department of the St John Ambulance First Aid service. I am now qualified to lead groups of First Aiders in a teaching environment and within First Aid competitions. These leadership skills will be useful in the future, as I will be able to work as part of a team and also make valuable individual contributions within this group environment. I am very much looking forward to the opportunities available to me at university; particularly the potential to become involved with community groups and student journalism.

My unwavering commitment to my studies and my dedication to an active and fulfilling extra-curricular timetable mean that I am an ideal candidate for your institution. I hope that I can expand upon the points made here at interview.

Example 34

The world's most remarkable writers, such as Shakespeare and his contemporaries, have been able to manipulate and influence readers' emotions and perceptions through their unique mastery of language and imagery. Encapsulating and reflecting back to us the essence of what it is to be human, they have the potential to induce in the reader a deeper and more sensitive exploration of the world and ourselves. By studying the ways in which skilled writers from different cultures and eras create personal links with readers which can cross centuries and languages requires us to consider the nature and complexities of humanity. My principal motivation in applying to study English is therefore to acquire the skills with which to critically examine how and why the experience of reading literature can touch our lives in such a personal way.

At an early age the vividly imaginative works of authors such as Lewis Carroll, CS Lewis and Roald Dahl captivated me. With maturity my taste has developed to include particular admiration for the Bronte sisters, the Pre-Raphaelites and the Italian-inspired creations of Robert Browning and Elizabeth Barrett Browning. I have also enjoyed studying translated classics such as the Greek tragedies and the works of Dante Alighieri. At university I hope to continue to widen my knowledge of different genres and in particular I look forward to further study of literature from the Renaissance, Gothic and Victorian periods, to exploring women's writing and to developing my own creative writing. Through studying these works I will also develop the critical faculty and experience to analyse further areas of literary interest in the future.

Since the age of 16, I have enjoyed the responsibility and independence brought about by combining full-time study with part-time work in various areas of the literary industry. As a Library Assistant, cataloguing, indexing and shelving reading material, I was taught the importance of a methodical and well-organised approach. Dealing with customer enquiries and working within a team of librarians, I also learned effective interpersonal skills and to respond efficiently to the needs of different individuals. Working as a bookseller, giving advice and recommendations, gave me further scope to share my enthusiasm for literature with others. In my current role as a Learning Support Assistant I find the children need to feel that they are being listened to and taken seriously, and to be spoken to in a manner which will engage and interest them, and utilise my listening and communicating skills accordingly. My employment has required me to devise effective time-management strategies, to adapt readily to new situations and people and to maintain a professional approach to meeting deadlines. Having completed a Pitman PA Diploma I have an excellent level of IT proficiency and am familiar with all the major Microsoft packages, skills I will implement when organising my study and designing presentations.

Volunteering as the co-ordinator of my most recent college's literary excursions, most of which were to outdoor Shakespeare productions by the Creation Theatre Company, involved encouraging both British and international students to attend these functions, arranging transport and playing 'host' for the evening. In leisure time I enjoy logic games such as chess, scrabble and draughts and I am an active member of a creative writing group. In the future I envisage myself encouraging an appreciation of literature within the public sector, either in education or as a chartered librarian. As a mature applicant with extensive experience I feel I will be entering higher education with a realistic appreciation of what it can offer, and I look forward to the challenges of a university degree.

Example 35

Both literature and language form central tenets of our culture and the development of society. Effective literature has the power to educate the reader, widening perspectives, challenging assumptions and providing a gateway to understanding different cultures, time periods and viewpoints. In pursuing English Language and Literature at university I hope to significantly widen my experience of literature whilst developing the critical skills and stylistic knowledge to evaluate texts effectively. Studying Language will also illuminate the impact of different tools used by writers and will teach me about the historical development of English within a wide context. As a future journalist this degree will familiarise me with language's role as a powerful medium for expressing ideas, information and opinions.

English Literature A level has been a fascinating opportunity to discover a wider range of authors and to explore their influences. Studying Shakespeare has demonstrated the impact of pushing the boundaries of contemporary linguistic standards and I have particularly valued the opportunity to formally study present day authors such as Jeanette Winterson and Roddy Doyle. Doyle's prolific use of 'free inner speech' as his principal narrative form complements his focus on everyday life and both he and Shakespeare perfectly illustrate the need to understand language in order to fully appreciate literature and in order to find a similarly distinctive voice as a writer oneself. Within English Language I have enjoyed experimenting with different frameworks through which to analyse and my understanding of both prescriptive and descriptive grammar has been deepened by the study of the language's development from Old English. Comparing theories of first language acquisition and innate language capacity has been one of my favourite elements of the course, complemented by Psychology AS. As I also spend much of my free time writing poetry, short stories and articles for the newspaper Nerd World and for the school newsletter, I am looking forward to joining relevant university societies and applying to be the editor of the student newspaper when eligible. I also hope to continue to develop my ability to articulately express my interpretations of a text and I will benefit from discussing texts with students from a wide variety of backgrounds and experiences. I am particularly keen to study the development of language and language acquisition in greater detail as well as to familiarise myself with literature from the renaissance to the present day.

Being a member of the student council since Year 7 has enhanced my organisational and teamwork skills whilst allowing me to contribute effectively to the school and, as well as participating in the debating society and book club, I am currently organising a Sixth Form literature club. Part time work as a sales assistant, waitress, and gallery assistant has allowed me to demonstrate my reliability, punctuality and leadership when training new staff, handling cash and working with people of all ages. Sporting activity, including running, kickboxing and representing my school in cross-country, allows me to keep fit and release stress. Last year I completed a work placement as an assistant copywriter at a communications company, writing articles and newsletters and contacting businesses in preparation for the Big Day Business Event 2009. This was an extremely valuable experience as, in addition to rapidly improving my interpersonal skills and confidence, it confirmed my commitment to a career in this sector. After graduation I intend to build my journalistic skills writing for newspapers and magazines before pursing my ultimate ambition of becoming a news reporter and I am confident that this degree programme will prepare me well for achieving these goals.

Environmental Studies

Example 36

Environmental Science attracts me as a varied and interdisciplinary degree program that will allow me to develop my interests in geography, biology and the natural world. I am also looking forward to gaining skills in field and laboratory research techniques that will help to prepare me for my future career in the environmental sector.

My combination of A level subjects has provided me with a strong background for progressing to Environmental Science. In Biology I have particularly enjoyed the components focusing on the structure and processes of plants and on the way in which all plants and animals have a crucial role to play in the ecosystem. For my coursework I compared the species diversity of an area of chalk down with a neighbouring area of managed parkland and this introduction to field studies motivated me to arrange work experience with my local Wildlife Trust. Studying Geography has given me an insight into the bigger picture of the planet's environments, and from Economics I have acquired a better understanding of conservation budgets and planning.

In all my subjects I have found the practical elements to be the most interesting part, as I enjoy putting theory into practice and I am looking forward to the field work requirements of this degree. In my own time I have been reading about the unique environments of the tropics and this is the area I wish to focus on as my specialism. During my year out I will be travelling with a conservation charity to the Eastern Arc Mountains of Tanzania to take part in a tropical forest expedition. The aim of the trip is to assist the scientists to record and survey the undocumented stretches of forest. For me it will be an opportunity to observe the kind of work I hope to become involved in after graduation and to discuss my career plans with others in the field. The expedition will be a once in a lifetime opportunity and I am already preparing by learning Swahili and reading back issues of 'African Wildlife' magazine.

For the past three years I have worked part time at a local DIY store as a customer service assistant. This role, dealing with customers' queries and complaints, has given me more confidence in my communication skills and my ability to think on my feet whilst responding to problems. During my year out I will be working here full time for six months in order to raise the money needed to go to Tanzania. Working at the Wildlife Trust once a month for the last 18 months has further developed my interpersonal skills as well as my understanding of the environment. Initially I spent each day there assisting the Ranger with land management work, building fences, planting hedges, thinning vegetation and other maintenance jobs. More recently I have begun working in the reception area, welcoming visitors and advising them on the best places to see different species on the reserve. In my leisure time I enjoy playing hockey matches and training with the school team, as well as attending local classical musical recitals. I am a self-motivated and hard working student, with a passion for environmentalism, and I look forward to the opportunities available to me at university.

Example 37

Since taking up scuba diving whilst in Australia three years ago, I have been fascinated by the marine environment. This is due to a combination of its physical beauty and complexity, its enormous size, covering over three-quarters of the Earth's surface, and the incredible fact that we have a more detailed knowledge of the surface of Mars than of the ocean. Since more has been discovered about marine ecosystems, people have begun to realise that despite its size it is not an inexhaustible or indestructible natural resource and that it needs as much protection as fragile areas of land. In the future I hope to be able to contribute to that protection as a specialist in the marine environment.

Over the last few years I have visited several marine aquariums and particularly enjoyed The Deep in Hull, where I attended a seminar on Threats to the Marine Environment. From my own reading, of books such as Mark Bertness's 'Marine Biology' and Robert Clark's 'Marine Pollution' I have supplemented my A levels with relevant knowledge. Biology and Geography have been my favourite subjects, especially when conducting experiments or research. For my Geography coursework this year, I am writing a report on the history of Britain's ports and I have enjoyed being able to learn about the effects of the marine environment on the ports' development, and how intertwined humans' lives have been with the sea. During my degree I am keen to build on my A level work and gain advanced skills in marine ecosystems, the effects of pollution, coastal navigation and oceanography. The chance to undertake fieldwork in tropical marine environments is a further attraction of this course.

This summer I worked with the Marine Conservation Society for two weeks in the Moray Firth in Scotland, promoting the charity and local events and helping with fundraising. As well as teaching me more about Marine Conservation, this helped to develop my confidence when speaking to new people and I enjoyed discussing campaigns with members of the public. In particular I was very interested to learn about the efforts to designate areas of offshore Britain as the first Marine National Park. I think this would be an important way to preserve Britain's heritage as an island nation and would help to protect areas from developments such as offshore energy projects and the expansion of the North Sea oilfields.

Working as a Plants Officer at a local garden centre has been useful in teaching me about practical aspects of plant growth such as reproduction and optimum growing conditions. This job involves working within a small team and I have learnt to co-operate with others, take instruction or use my initiative where appropriate, and present a professional attitude to customers who ask me for advice. Much of my free time is taken up by practising and performing with my school choir and orchestra, in which I play percussion. We recently competed in the National Festival of Music for Youth at the Festival Hall in London and I enjoy the camaraderie of these trips and the chance to visit different parts of the country. I have been scuba diving for several years and also enjoy water-skiing and sailing. My ambitions are to work within marine environmental science and at the moment I am intending to continue with further study after I graduate. I consider myself a well rounded and hardworking student, with a range of academic and musical interests, and I look forward to meeting the challenges of life and study at university.

Film Studies

Example 38

Through taking a degree in Film Studies I am hoping to broaden my knowledge of film culture, to examine the relationship of film with other aspects of visual culture and also to develop my own skills in photography and film making. In the future I am hoping to have a film career myself and I am looking forward to learning about the history of the industry.

At school I have enjoyed Media Studies A level because of the opportunities it has given me to explore the different elements of our culture, such as television, film and advertising. In particular I enjoyed discussing theories such as film discourse, and I am finding my coursework on the language used in advertising very interesting. At university, I am excited about having the opportunity to discuss such theories with fellow students who share some of my interests and to learn from their experiences and views. Whilst studying English Literature I have found Shakespeare's plays fascinating, both in terms of the language and characterisation used and in terms of the enduring popularity of the stories he created. For my English coursework I am completing a piece of extended writing on the modern day appeal of Shakespeare, including speculation on whether any film makers of the past hundred years will have the same impact on society in the future. I have also enjoyed using different techniques of stylistic analysis to discover the ways in which authors and poets convey their ideas and I am confident this skill will transfer usefully to analysing the film director's craft. Physics A level has helped to give me a more rounded academic experience and modules such as Optics, in which we constructed a camera and used different lenses and lighting techniques, have been relevant to my interest in film.

As well as practising filmmaking and photography at home, I enjoy reading about film history in my own time. Recently I have been studying the films of the classical Hollywood era, such as 'The Big Sleep' and 'Citizen Kane', as well as the social context in which the films were created and received. I am looking forward to studying topics such as this at university, as well as performance and editing, at a much higher level. More than anything I am excited about learning the critical skills to evaluate and analyse films in ways which will help me in my own future filmmaking.

When I am not indulging my interest in film, I regularly join my local mountaineering club for rock climbing trips in the Peak District. Having been climbing since I was ten I find it to be an excellent way to relax as it requires so much physical effort and mental concentration that it is impossible to worry about anything else. I will soon be taking my Single Pitch Award and I hope to continue climbing, and hopefully to have the opportunity to join expeditions abroad at university. I am intending to undertake further practical training in film after I graduate but I am confident that this degree will give me a rigorous academic understanding of the film industry from which to pursue my career.

Example 39

Film Studies appeals to me as it will allow me to combine my enjoyment of popular culture and performance, with a theoretical understanding of how the film industry fits into the wider culture of a society and of how the industry has progressed since its beginning in the 19th century.

Having thoroughly enjoyed the study of Art History at A level, I am very keen to continue to study an aspect of visual culture at university. During Art History I have found it especially interesting to build up an overview, through AS and A2, of the development of Renaissance art through the early modern period and of the development of Modernism in the 20th century. Appreciating that Renaissance art came at a time of great societal change and advances in science and technology, and that Modernism had a backdrop of war and further scientific developments, has helped me to understand the meaning intended by the artists, as well as contemporary interpretations. Studying the wider movements of art and of critical theory has allowed me to understand individual works of art more fully and I am hoping to gain a similar overview of film history from this degree, which will then help me to analyse individual films in context. Another aspect of Art History that has interested me is the question of authorship and readership. For my coursework I looked at the different ways in which one painting, Da Vinci's 'The Last Supper', has been interpreted through history and the effect the audience's cultural background has on how they view it. I am very keen to study the modules on this topic at university, as the issue of whether a film should be interpreted primarily in terms of the 'author' or the 'reader' is very interesting to me, requiring the study of the gender, class, sexuality and ethnicity of the 'reader'.

In my other A levels I have enjoyed practical work, particularly the opportunity to design a piece and then see it through from my imagination to the final creation. In both Art and Graphic Design I have been introduced to many of the styles, such as trompe l'oeil and pointillism, used by the artists I have studied in Art History. It has also been fascinating to learn how developments in the making of paints and dyes influenced the types of art that could be created. In the Film History module I will be interested to see how developments in CGI and other special effects have influenced which films have been made and also whether a technique being novel, such as the use of CGI in 'Toy Story', increases the popularity of a film.

Being a year representative at college has given me the chance to prove myself as a responsible member of the school community and I have enjoyed being in a position to help my fellow students. This year I am also assisting with a new 'buddy' project which aims to make new students more at home in their first few weeks by pairing them with a final year student. Helping with this has made me more aware of the problems faced by some students, and how simple things such as a buddy system can help, and I would like to become involved in the Students' Union at university, perhaps as a student counsellor or a Nightline volunteer. In the future I am hoping to work in education, passing on my enthusiasm for the arts to others, and I am confident that the skills and expertise I will gain at university will assist me in this goal.

Finance

Example 40

In studying Finance I am hoping to build upon my enjoyment of applied maths to help improve people's standard of living through a stronger economy. This is particularly important in countries such as my own, Lithuania, which are still trying to develop their economic stability and which suffer from a lack of suitably trained professionals. Through studying this degree I hope to gain relevant expertise and ideas from one of the world's strongest economies, which I can then return home with to help Lithuania's development.

At school I have enjoyed studying Maths, in particular, how it can be usefully applied to the real world as in business, finance and accounting. The need for logical problem solving skills attracts me to areas such as algebra, trigonometry and calculus, especially when it is necessary to use several different approaches before a solution can be found. Throughout school I have competed successfully in many Maths Olympiads and have always considered it a hobby as well as study. In addition to completing projects in how to understand Maths better, I have enjoyed sharing my enthusiasm for the subject with other pupils who are having difficulties. Studying for a Junior Achievement Diploma in Economics has given me a strong introduction to the subject, including how to write business plans and analyse investment risks. I have particularly enjoyed learning about the differences between micro and macroeconomics and the relationship between them. At university I am keen to develop this understanding of economics, accountancy and the financial world further and to learn how to use appropriate theories to critically evaluate different case study scenarios. I am also looking forward to studying the history and development of finance and accountancy, and their growing importance to the wider economy of a country.

At school I have been an active student and was part of a youth group called Pozemis which campaigned to improve our city's economy through various projects. After researching our options we concluded tourism was the best way to develop the area so we made links with a partner youth club in Belgium and exchanged ideas to help promote tourism. I have also helped to promote Lithuanian culture by travelling across Europe as part of a competitive dance group, which was ranked first in the country three years running, and as a member of a choir which has also been placed first nationally. Winning first prize as part of a team in a 'Students Against Aids and Drugs' contest, in which we produced presentations to highlight these dangers, helped to develop my skills in research, teamwork and communication. In English speaking I have been awarded first place in inter-regional competitions, and I came second in the 'Temide' Law competition. As class president I was responsible for organising cultural and educational activities for students, improving my leadership qualities and allowing me to contribute to the school community.

In my leisure time I enjoy travelling and experiencing new cultures and languages, reading a variety of literature, and organising cultural festivals. At university I intend to involve myself fully in student activities and societies and perhaps to take up some new hobbies. I also hope to make the most of my time there to gain extensive work experience in the financial sector, in order to prepare myself fully for a career in this industry. I am a determined and hardworking student, who works diligently and without complaint and will bring this committed attitude with me to university.

Example 41

Economic activity is a fundamental aspect of modern society, with a significant impact on everything from an individual's financial circumstances to a country's domestic development and foreign policy. As my future goal is to work within the financial industry, I now wish to study a degree in this area at university, gaining the knowledge and crucial skills for success in my chosen career.

At A level I have found Economics a fascinating subject, particularly studying supply and demand and understanding the advantages and disadvantages of free trade to developing countries such as my own. Macroeconomic policies and the impact of issues such as inflation and unemployment on a country's economic development also interest me and have helped me to understand the complexity of the problems countries such as Pakistan are dealing with. I have always enjoyed exploring the issues faced by the world around me, and self-directed reading of relevant literature, such as The Economist, allows me to keep up to date with my knowledge. Business Studies has helped me to develop the skills to effectively evaluate and analyse different situations and through numerous projects and presentations I have also developed my leadership and communication skills. Accounting and Maths have provided me with an academic challenge that has complemented my other subjects and developed my advanced numeracy and problem solving skills. This combination of studies has allowed me to become more flexible in identifying the most appropriate solutions to different economic problems. My academic efforts have been rewarded with the Breton Medal for Maths and the Principal's Medal for Pakistan Studies and Urdu, and I intend to bring the same level of commitment to my University studies. I enjoy tackling new challenges and look forward to taking increasing responsibility for my academic development.

Weekend work managing my family's business has given me practical experience of business practices and introduced me to the basics of sales, advertising, resource management and bookkeeping. It has given me ample opportunity to interact with customers, developing my interpersonal skills, and has provided a context to my economic studies. Voluntary work teaching Maths and English to children from deprived backgrounds was an enlightening experience, helping me to truly appreciate the opportunity I have to attend university. Mentoring physically and mentally disabled children requires excellent interpersonal and caring skills and the ability to respond differently to each child depending on their needs. Organising regular fundraising events and my role as treasurer of various school societies has helped me to improve my initiative, organisational skills and sense of responsibility. I have relished contributing to the school community and made good use of effective time management techniques to ensure I can meet my academic and extra-curricular activities. In my leisure time I find my involvement in tennis, squash and water sports helps me to unwind and keep physically and mentally agile. I have won 2nd prize in a school photography competition and I find this hobby helps me to see things from different angles. Performing in school drama productions has improved my confidence, and the guitar and sketching provide further creative outlets. Extensive European travel has broadened my perspective on life and I enjoy meeting people from different cultural backgrounds.

In the future I hope to continue my studies at Masters level before working towards a career in financial consultancy or starting my own business and I am confident this degree will equip me with the skills and expertise required to embark upon this path. I am a well-rounded and self-disciplined student and I look forward to making full use of the opportunities, both academic and personal, available to me at university.

Forensics

Example 42

Since beginning a part time job at a hospital laboratory, maintaining hygiene and cleanliness whilst making use of the opportunity to talk to the scientists, I have been very interested in studying an applied science at university. After researching my options I am attracted to the investigative aspect and direct relevance to wider society of Forensic Science.

The range of areas of science involved in forensics, such as pharmacology, toxicology, ecology, cell biology and statistical science is fascinating, as is the interaction between these different fields. Having been interested in the story of the child's torso found in the Thames in 2001, I have recently been reading several articles about it. I have found the way in which forensic scientists identified his geographical origin from pollen in his stomach which traced him to Africa, and used his bone isotope signature to narrow the area down to a small part of Nigeria, compelling motivation for gaining these skills myself. As the relevant technology develops to allow more and more sophisticated analysis forensic science will play an increasingly important role in providing evidence for trials and I look forward to playing a part in this research.

As well as my job at the hospital laboratory I have completed a work placement at a solicitors' firm, where I learnt about many of the legal issues surrounding giving evidence which will be effective in court. I also had the opportunity to observe a Barrister in two different trials, including one in which a forensic scientist gave evidence regarding the nature of a victim's injuries. Working at the laboratory has allowed me to see some of the content of my Science A levels applied to real life situations, and has brought topics such as anatomy and pharmacology to life for me. As well as the relevant scientific expertise, I look forward to acquiring the skills to use scientific equipment, and ICT tools, to implement my knowledge effectively.

My holiday job in a supermarket has required me to work alongside people of a range of ages and backgrounds and to deal with customer enquiries in a professional and courteous manner, developing my interpersonal and communication skills. Playing for the First XV rugby team I have developed skills in teamwork and co-operation, and have had the opportunity to travel, such as on a recent tour of Ireland. Training five times a week, and playing two matches a week in season, has taught me the value of hard work and dedication when working towards specific goals. Out of season I enjoy playing football, squash and badminton. As a member of the Cadet Force for a year I enjoyed the focus on fitness, self-discipline and leadership. Flying also occupies much of my leisure time and I will be applying for my pilot's licence shortly. To date this year I have flown eight times, and attended a week long Pilot Induction course.

In the future I envisage myself working within a forensic science laboratory, perhaps supporting the police service. In the long term I would like to contribute to the continued development of forensic science research. My degree will provide me with the knowledge and practical skills to embark on this career path and I look forward to the challenges of living and studying at university.

Example 43

Forensic Science is a vital part of the justice system and in pursuing a career in this area I hope to apply my enjoyment of science to public health and public safety. At school my favourite topics have been in Physics, Chemistry and Maths, particularly Statistics. Most of all I am interested in genetics and how this can be used to identify victims and suspects. Whilst studying Forensic Science I am looking forward to understanding how DNA profiling can be used to match a sample of blood to a fragment of hair, for example, as well as to the use of IT in this process. Having completed work experience with the police service I have become aware of some of the ethical issues surrounding the use of profiling, such as the recent move towards profiling every prisoner charged with a serious offence, and maintaining a DNA database, as is currently done in parts of Scotland. I have also been fascinated to learn of the possible implications of scientific and technological developments on decades-old unsolved cases.

In order to confirm my career interests I have recently attended a week long placement with the police service, in which I was introduced to different areas such as dog handling, traffic and firearms. This has been important in allowing me to understand the wider criminal justice system and the role of forensics within it. In my spare time I enjoy keeping up to date with developments and debates in science through journals such as New Scientist and Nature. Recently I have been enjoying an ongoing debate in these publications regarding the extent to which the current popularity of television shows featuring forensic scientists may jeopardise their work. This is partly because jurors have inaccurate expectations of the forensic expert's role in a court hearing, but also because of the possibility of criminals becoming increasingly forensically aware.

Fulfilling my duties as a Senior Prefect I have enjoyed utilising my initiative, diplomacy and communication skills to assist teachers and staff in the smooth running of the school. Working as a shop assistant has required strong interpersonal skills and the ability to maintain a professional and tactful manner when dealing with difficult customers. I have enjoyed this opportunity to meet and work with many different people and I have benefited from the financial and personal independence associated with having a part-time job.

In order to work to my full academic potential a good balance of leisure activities is essential. With my local riding club I participate in both team and individual competitions in show-jumping. Team events have given me the opportunity to develop my leadership, supporting and motivating the other riders. In order to compete individually I train and practise frequently and have learnt the value of persistence and determination in improving my performance. I have also been involved backstage in several productions and have performed on stage in several plays including a recent production of Romeo and Juliet. Combining my hobbies with maintaining high academic standards has demanded good time management and prioritising of responsibilities, and I intend to bring the same level of commitment to both my academic and extra-curricular activities at university.

Geography

Example 44

Geography has many facets, and it is the variety of topics offered in the course that make the study of Geography exceptionally attractive. I also find the history of human Geography interesting because of the way it has influenced, and is being experienced by, modern society. I wish to pursue a career in Climatology because this has become an increasingly important and developing field within the past few decades. My interest in Geography has been long-standing, and I am particularly interested in climate change and Biogeography. I have a hard-working attitude, together with a desire to succeed, that would serve me well in successfully completing a course in Geography.

I chose to study Biology, Geography and Chemistry at A level due to my interest in Science. I feel these subjects will enhance my interest and learning ability in Geography by encouraging me to think logically, analytically and with reason. Through Chemistry I have become practised in evaluating evidence and drawing conclusions whilst Biology has given me an in depth appreciation of natural processes. In June 2010 I undertook work experience at an environmental consultancy firm, and I gained invaluable experience in issues such as waste management, environmental impact assessments and land management. I regularly read 'Chemistry Review' magazine and have taken part in various Geography seminars, a testament to my excellent independent studying skills.

I am currently working towards my Duke of Edinburgh Silver Award and taking part in a Young Enterprise company as Finance Director, in order to learn about the importance of teamwork as well as accountancy skills. A further part entailed helping GCSE students learn German, whereby I developed my skills in recognising and addressing other peoples' needs. I believe that these skills are particularly useful in the varied careers which a degree in Geography can lead to. In August 2011 I am going on a Raleigh International trip to Romania, exploring the country and taking part in charity work. I hope to gain insight into another culture and way of life, using it primarily as a self-building activity. To finance this I am working in the Health Records Department at my local hospital. The work involves patient confidentiality and enables me to meet and work with people of all ages and races, thus helping me to develop good interpersonal and communication skills; all of which are essential for the study of Geography.

One of the many social activities I enjoy is leading a water aerobics class once a week in my local sports centre, as well as playing first bassoon in my regional Youth Orchestra. I regularly participate in both regional and school concerts. I have an interest in sport and swim regularly, attend yoga classes and play tennis with friends. I especially enjoy going to the theatre and reading books. I have given a lot of consideration to choosing a degree course that I will enjoy, that I am utterly suited to, and that I can assure one hundred percent commitment to, however long it may take to complete. I am looking forward to the challenge and stimulation of university life and the career benefits that a good degree in Geography would bring.

Example 45

My keen sense of curiosity and interest in the world around me has been underpinned through completing the academically rigorous International Baccalaureate and its encouragement of social responsibility and performing arts. I see Geography as the logical further step to continuing my academic studies.

As part of my IB I have completed an extended essay in Geography on Tourism in Mallorca, which discussed cultural attitudes, and also spent time in Morocco on a field trip which looked at different lifestyles and attitudes. I have enjoyed the human element and cultural issues which have been a theme of most of my subjects. These have confirmed my interest in Human Geography. At university I am looking forward to expanding my limited knowledge of Environmental Geography. Studying Mathematics has given me problem-solving and analytical skills whilst completing my extended essay has given me the freedom and self-motivation of independent research. Overall, the IB has taught me to work consistently and to manage deadlines, thus enabling me to complete large volumes of work. These are valuable transferable skills I can take with me to university.

Having managed epilepsy since the age of seven, I am shortly to experience a major change of medication. In order to forward-plan and to ensure that my condition is stable prior to commencing my university studies, I am deferring my application. During this period I plan to work in the City to finance a period of travel. Having travelled within Europe, I intend to travel further afield and experience different cultures to prepare me for my future studies.

As part of my IB community service, I have spent time teaching music to primary school children. This has enhanced my communication skills and shown me I have the skills to put across ideas in a friendly and understandable way. Sometimes this required initiative and for me to be fairly adaptable in my approach. Work experience for an insurance company in a number of differing areas has shown me how people interact at work and improved my interpersonal skills. It also gave me the opportunity of expanding my computer skills. I particularly enjoyed my time in the human resources department through observing their recruitment process to their staff appraisal scheme. Inspired by my time there, my ambition is to work in HR management as I am at my best with people and enjoy supporting others.

As a school prefect, I have responsibility for supervising younger children and this has developed my leadership skills. At school, as a music scholar, I have achieved Flute Grade 7, Piano Grade 6, Singing Grade 7 and Music Theory Grade 6. Being Lead Flautist with the Dulwich Youth Orchestra required me to have excellent time management skills and to be very well organised to ensure a balance with my academic studies. Music is both a source of enjoyment and relaxation; I both perform and listen to music of all genres. Representing my school at hockey and netball has been very rewarding. In order to improve my physical fitness and stamina, I undertook training and am now a qualified lifeguard. In my spare time I enjoy a good social life and enjoy reading for pleasure.

At university I intend to continue my extra-curricular activities, in both music and sport, in order to make friends and also to offset the inevitable stress of university life. I am an ambitious and highly motivated student and I am looking forward to the challenges and personal rewards of studying for my university degree.

History

Example 46

The discipline of History is vital to the development and progression of society as a whole. Without the benefit of hindsight and retrospection, the modern world would not have the complexity and divisions in areas of politics, religion, economics, communication and social status. Indeed, some would argue that civilisation could not adapt without the lessons from history. This is why History fascinates me as a subject and why I am eager to delve further into its intricacies.

The poetry of Siegfried Sassoon and Wilfred Owen has particularly intrigued me in both my History and English courses. These writings encompass the many layers of the Great War and highlight the contradictions between patriotism and the gruesome realities of changing modern warfare. Academically, my analytical understanding of History has developed through the study of Tudor history. Historical texts including 'Children of England' by Alison Weir, 'Elizabeth and Mary' by Jane Dunn and 'Bloody Mary's Martyrs' by Jasper Ridley have influenced my opinions of this period. Although the reign of Queen Mary was a brutal one, I have, however, become enthralled by her religious motivations. This, of course, has definite parallels with religious tolerance in the modern world. The notions of traditionalist and revisionist History allow the subject to continuously evolve.

In 2010, I was awarded the Thomas Moore Scholarship for two years for my contribution to school life. This was a great honour and has enabled me to consolidate a variety of skills and interests. The analytical skills I have acquired through my interest in History have been transferred into my fulfilling extra-curricular activities. As the debating and public speaking captain, I have a genuine interest in forming and sustaining arguments. I relish the opportunity to debate topics. I am responsible for organising and participating in a range of events, including the Mace debate and the ESU competition. My leadership abilities are evident in my role as Head of Fisher House. This has allowed me to become a very strong person with excellent social skills that have only added to my self-motivated, organised and independent character at boarding school. I was an NHVS leader, which is a voluntary group in our school that looks after elderly people in the local community. As a school librarian, organisation is intrinsic within my character. I believe wholly in experiencing all I can from university life.

Education is the key to progress. This principle became clear to me when I worked with communities in Honduras this summer with World Challenge organisations. We taught the children English and made practical repairs to the local school. It was through these impoverished children that the value and importance of learning became obvious. This was confirmed again when I undertook work experience as a classroom assistant in a local prep school. These experiences have provided me with a long term goal of working in Education. Making a difference to children's lives must be the most valuable reward of all.

As a student I would be committed to university both academically and socially. I am especially looking forward to participating in the dancing and the sailing clubs because it will enable me to further my hobbies. The characteristics I have developed to date mean that I am a dedicated, positive and involved individual. I wish to embrace the opportunity of a successful and fulfilling life at university. The interests and rewards History offers at degree level will enrich my understanding of society and empower me to make a difference in the future.

Example 47

The study of History has had a profound impact on my perception of the world, allowing me a deeper understanding of humanity, of global politics and of the importance of tolerance and respect in diplomacy. The social and political evolution of the ancient civilisations, and how they compare to the modern world, is particularly fascinating. Having supplemented my school work with independent reading and numerous visits to museums and exhibitions I now wish to increase my knowledge of the subject further.

During my A levels I have enjoyed debating the controversial theories surrounding the issue of responsibility for the atrocities of Nazi Germany and Soviet Russia. Being selected to attend a course at Auschwitz during the Holocaust commemorations was a deeply moving experience. As well as highlighting the importance of respect for diversity it has made me feel strongly about the need to confront racism and intolerance wherever it is found. The importance of religion was also made apparent during a Sociology project in which I examined the significance of religion in modern society, and I am keen to learn how the changing religions of ancient Rome affected their society.

My love of history has been fuelled by trips to the ancient Olympia site, Rome's ruins, and a museum about the Etruscans which focused on their trade links with other countries, highlighting the pre-Roman cultural exchange across Europe. Recently I visited the British Museum's Ancient Persia exhibition where visitors can use the Iranian artefacts to discover how they saw themselves rather than relying on the Greeks' interpretations. It also cast some light on the history of current Middle Eastern issues. Reading History Today and The Economist helps me to broaden my knowledge and I am also interested in public history, especially the treatment of ancient history in recent movies such as Gladiator and Troy.

At the Surrey History Centre I cleaned and catalogued Roman tiles and greatly enjoyed discussing theories about the Romans with the archaeologists. I also volunteered at a dig near Godstone which gave me a fascinating insight into the habits and migratory patterns of local Neolithic people. During my gap year in South America I will study the Inca ruins and help with conservation work nearby. This will be an unforgettable experience and I look forward to the challenges of living in a foreign country and meeting new people.

As History Captain I have encouraged Year 9 pupils to pursue history, which helped me develop my initiative and sense of responsibility. I have also increased my research and communication skills by delivering presentations and making wall displays on the 60th anniversary of D-Day. Gaining a distinction for my role in a Young Enterprise team, I improved my administrative skills writing minutes and organising a sales event. Tutoring a Year 7 pupil in Maths has been very rewarding as his confidence and ability have increased significantly through my support. Work at a Cancer Research shop, for my Duke of Edinburgh Silver Award, has improved my interpersonal skills considerably as I work with colleagues of all ages and am constantly serving the public.

Aside from my interest in History, I am active in several clubs and societies. These include Politics and Chess, in which I have won first place in various tournaments. In skiing I am proud to have recently achieved intermediate level and I intend to continue with these hobbies at university. Following my degree I am considering continuing my studies with an MA or PhD, which will allow me to continue to develop my passion for the subject.

International Relations

Example 48

My motivation to study International Relations is my interest in the history and processes of global diplomatic relations, and the impact they can have on the economic and political development of a country. With a future career in international politics in mind I wish to gain specialist knowledge of the current and past state of international relations and equip myself with the necessary skills in critical analysis, research and evaluation of information, and communication. After a temporary break from education whilst having my daughter, I am now taking my A levels and am in a position to commit myself fully to a university degree.

Taking A level intensive courses has been an engaging return to learning. In Psychology I most enjoy studying 'Obedience and Conformity' as I find society's tendency to conservatism and conformity fascinating. I feel that my background in this area will give me a different perspective on international politics, looking at the humans behind the diplomatic decisions and their personal and psychological reasons for responding to situations in particular ways. In Philosophy I find studying the philosophy of the mind particularly interesting as it explores our knowledge, assumptions and perceptions of ourselves and the world. Again, I feel that these areas have strong resonances in the world of politics.

My interest in both domestic and international politics is longstanding and, having often felt frustrated by political inaction or apathy, I am keen to gain detailed knowledge of the subject before getting personally involved through future employment. At university I am looking forward to studying the working of the international community, and how events such as conflict and foreign policy can impact on this. Topics such as foreign policy analysis especially appeal to me as they will provide me with the tools to critically evaluate the policies of different countries and to understand the ways in which they are developed and implemented. In particular I hope to increase my understanding of the interconnections at all levels of domestic policy and international political situations, as well as topical areas such as international security, which plays an increasing role in determining foreign policy and the integration of international systems. I also intend to take full advantage of the opportunity to study and complete work placements abroad, preparing myself fully for the graduate job market.

Living in two very different countries, Ghana and the USA, has complemented my interest in the international system, demonstrating the varying but equally valid needs of different communities and cultures. Spending time in Africa has also ensured I am fully appreciative of my education and the opportunities available to me. My experience of the challenges of being a young single parent has been a further contributor to my personal growth, and has provided extra impetus to my desire to ensure good prospects for both my child and myself. As well as this high level of commitment, parenthood has required strong abilities in time management and prioritising in order to combine it successfully with my A level studies. In my leisure time I enjoy sports and played for my college netball team. I also enjoy the creative outlet of my own writing, particularly short stories, and I look forward to continuing with these interests at university.

In the future I envisage myself completing a Masters degree, before hopefully working within the UN. To date I have worked extremely hard to make the best of my educational opportunities and I am fully committed to achieving the same high standards at university, preparing myself for a successful career in international relations.

Example 49

I find the current world political scene and its effect on the worldwide development of human rights particularly interesting, which makes International Relations a fascinating degree to study in the current geopolitical climate. Especially recently, with developments in information technology, the economic and political growth of India and China, and current issues of terrorism and nuclear proliferation, I think that now it is both an exciting and challenging time to study this area.

My chosen A level subjects of History, English and Sociology reflect my academic interests, particularly socio-linguistics and political history. Studying Business at AS level improved my knowledge of organisations and the business world. I am capable with computers and learned the fundamentals of programming, allowing me to further develop this ability at college in computing lessons. English has allowed me to develop my love for original writing and creative work and in studying History I have been able to further develop my analytical skills and ability to form coherent arguments to support different viewpoints.

I am a keen sportsman, with my favourite sports being tennis, football and field athletics. I play tennis at least once a week in the winter and almost everyday in the summer, belonging to two teams: my local village and my local town. I enjoy tennis squad training in which there is an emphasis on technique and style and have attended squad training for six years. I much prefer to play well and lose than to win whilst playing badly, because I get more enjoyment from pulling off a successful and well-executed shot than I do from looking at a statistic on a sheet.

With a strong social conscience and a passion for writing and communication, I undertook unpaid work experience on a local paper. I gained a wide exposure to a number of journalistic duties, including interviewing, research, proofreading and copy writing, all of which will stand me in excellent stead to realise my ultimate career aim of writing on cultural and political issues, both nationally and internationally. I regularly read publications such as The New Statesman, The Economist and The Spectator in order to keep myself up-to-date with current affairs, and also to immerse myself in the writing style of my chosen form of journalism.

I have a sense of social obligation, illustrated by my role in the organisation of a health conference for my year group which aimed to inform students on drugs, contraception and independent living, along with developing awareness of the Law regarding sexual offences and encouraging empathy towards victims. I was involved in the eight-month planning process: discussing with various professionals what we would like to see covered in the workshops, writing questionnaires to get student input, producing posters to advertise it, and also helping to ensure that things ran smoothly on the day. I also participated in a paired-reading scheme in which I helped a younger student with reading difficulties to improve his reading age and ability, whilst I also put in many hours helping to run and umpire tennis matches for younger students as part of a Community Sports Leaders Award. My involvement in these activities developed my organisational and communication skills, and I also felt great pride in the fact that I had done something really worthwhile.

I believe that I am an adaptable, articulate and well-rounded student with the necessary drive and application to thrive both academically and socially at university. International Relations is particularly suited to both my academic strengths and my personality attributes; I am fair, confident and always determined to succeed in everything that I undertake.

Languages

Example 50

My motivation to study French and Spanish comes from my lifelong fascination with learning and comparing foreign languages and cultures. Having thoroughly enjoyed my study of A level French, and as a Korean immigrant having become fluent in English over the last five years, I wish to continue to develop my linguistic ability.

In studying Languages I am particularly interested in the insight they give into the culture and society of the people using them. Researching French A level projects, I have enjoyed learning the traditions and history of Provence and of France in general. I encountered French for the first time in Year 9 and was pleased to progress quickly enough to achieve an A at GCSE. My native language is Korean, and I am fluent in written and conversational English, so I am looking forward to adding to this by learning Spanish from scratch. This will also provide a gateway to learning more about Spain and particularly Latin America, an area I find fascinating. The opportunity to explore the nature of language itself, through the study of linguistics, is also very appealing.

Having spent a total of 13 weeks in France, at language schools and staying with a French family, I have seen the importance of full immersion to learn a language well. For this reason I am very excited about spending a year of my degree in a different country. Whilst living and studying in France I not only furthered my French skills but also my adaptability and confidence in communicating with people of all ages. I feel making the effort to learn the relevant language when travelling is important in developing strong relationships with individuals, as well as between countries.

As Senior Prefect I supervised other prefects and assisted the staff with the smooth running of the school, showing strong leadership and providing a good role model for other pupils. Taking part in a Young Enterprise team was very rewarding and it demonstrated the need for effective teamwork and good listening skills when debating the opinions of the whole group. My interest in business also led me to be a regional finalist of the Pro-Share Young Investors scheme. This developed my public speaking skills and the ability to debate and deliver my ideas and opinions coherently. Involvement in the Charity Club has been an excellent way to contribute to society and has required a high level of organisation and time management to co-ordinate fundraising.

Working part-time in a clothing shop, I have used my interpersonal skills when dealing with customers, co-workers and managers and my initiative when dealing with customer queries. Through completing my Bronze and Silver Duke of Edinburgh Awards, I have gained new skills and worked with many new people. I expect to complete my Gold in due course. First Aid training has helped me to learn how to stay calm and focused when under pressure. I am a qualified Rescue Diver, complemented by my First Aid skills, and I play on the Rugby A Team. Practising the guitar, I have seen the value of persistence and commitment in achieving goals and I am also enjoying learning Japanese in my free time. My four years of altar service at Plymouth Cathedral have given me great personal satisfaction, assisting the Dean and the Bishop.

Inspired by my enjoyment of the Young Enterprise and Pro-Share schemes, I am considering making use of my language skills by working in international business. I am a hardworking and dedicated student, with a strong commitment to my subject and an active extra-curricular life, and I feel I have the qualities to make a positive contribution to the university.

Example 51

Most potential university students can pinpoint an exact event at which they realised what their true academic calling in life was. Personally, I can trace my interest in languages back to a holiday to the Lleyn Peninsula when I was six, during which I decided to compile a dictionary of the Welsh words I saw on signposts. My interest gained ground at secondary school, and in recent years I have become particularly enthusiastic about the language and culture of Spain – an enthusiasm heightened by a visit to Galicia last summer. While I am enjoying A level French I am keen to take the opportunity of some free time in the timetable to learn something new, hence my desire to study Italian. Italy is a country which fascinates me and which I would love to get to know, and I already have some knowledge of the language including the pronunciation system.

Last term I took part in a French essay-writing competition organised by the Alliance Francaise, and for my essay on Globalisation I was awarded a Certificat d'Or. Last year also saw my participation in the school French Exchange, which I found a valuable insight into French culture as well as a chance to improve my language. Apart from my French and Spanish studies, I have pursued other languages at various times. Last year I took the one-year GCSE course in Latin that my school offers, which I have found very interesting and highly worthwhile and it has given me an insight into Romance languages. Out of enthusiasm for the west of Scotland and interest in Scottish place-names I have learnt some Gaelic, and I recently started to teach myself German.

I have been elected Deputy Head Boy with responsibility for charity for this year, and in this position I hope to continue the impressive fund-raising efforts of previous years for local and national causes. I have successfully completed my Gold Duke of Edinburgh Award, for which I took up rock-climbing and helped residents in a local nursing home. I am an active First Aider, having taken part in regional and national First Aid competitions with the St. John Ambulance. I am on the committee of the Debating Society and have spoken in a number of debates in the Society's first year; through school I have also taken part in a public speaking competition organised by the Rotary Club, for which I spoke as part of a team of three on 'How we will view life in the next millennium.' I am a keen actor, and have had leading roles in productions both in and out of school. In my spare time I enjoy orienteering and photography, as well as reading (especially travel writing) and playing the mouth organ, for which my main interest is the traditional music of Scotland and Northumberland.

As for my future plans, I am strongly considering interpreting as a career; I think I would find this work very interesting, and I feel I can meet the challenge it presents. In the meantime I am looking forward to starting my university course and to the new experiences it will offer me.

Law

Example 52

My fascination with Law stems from its function as the foundation of all aspects of a society. During my Anthropology degree, I have studied the cultural origins of the beliefs and assumptions on which laws are based and the power which rests in these laws, and often fuels inequalities across the globe. My intention is to further my education in this area in order to better equip myself to address some of the most persistent inequalities.

My current degree is based on a holistic programme giving the student an extensive education in the field before choosing a specialism. My particular interest has been in Globalisation and its far-reaching impact on all levels of society. However I also studied topics such as Molecular Genetics and Cultural Violence, making the most of the diversity of information available to me. The multidisciplinary nature of Law appeals to me in a similar manner and I look forward to learning the basics of the entire legal system from tort to family law. My real passion however, is for understanding the criminal justice system. Further to this I am fascinated by the concept and realities of International Law and its authority over nation states. After early involvement in debating contests, relishing the situation of being encouraged to argue, my interest in Law increased significantly after the controversial election which brought George W. Bush to office. I see my pursuit of Law as an ongoing battle to seek the truth in order to reduce corruption, injustice and the associated tragedies. In applying to UK institutions I hope to have the opportunity of studying at internationally renowned Law Schools; I am in the habit of aiming high and striving to achieve these goals.

At college I was elected President of the Student Council which involved addressing the concerns of the student population and organising events. This developed my interpersonal skills as I liaised between staff and students, and demanded managerial and leadership qualities which I found came naturally to me. As a member of the Prefect Board I helped to create a bridge between the Council, staff and local community, and organised fundraisers, food drives and humanitarian projects. Teaching students about the Islamic faith, I enjoyed encouraging them in expressing and discussing their views on current issues. Coaching basketball gave me a similar sense of satisfaction as I taught the children rules and techniques of the game alongside sportsmanship. I have also worked as a basketball referee, upholding the rules and remaining impartial.

As a student I received a Gold Medal in the Calgary City Science Fair, and Awards of Excellence in Maths and Spanish. After four years at university I have established a system of time management and balancing my academic and extra-curricular activities. As well as my interests in travel and humanitarianism I am an active sportsman. Amateur boxing, in which I am Canadian Junior Welterweight Champion, and Regional and Provincial Lightweight Champion, occupies much of my spare time and has shown me the value of persistence, commitment and positivity in achieving results. I also participate in Varsity rugby, soccer and basketball, and I intend to continue with these and other sports at university in the UK.

In the long term I would like to run my own practice and ultimately, having acquired sufficient experience, to use my expertise to found humanitarian projects around the world. As an active and well-rounded student, with diverse interests and a genuine passion for studying Law, I feel I have the attributes required to make the most of the opportunities available at university.

Example 53

In pursuing a Law degree, I look forward to analysing the precedents and controversies which have contributed to our legal system and shaped society. I feel I will benefit from learning critical thinking and developing my capacity for problem solving and constructing logical arguments.

In school I am a conscientious and inquisitive student and have recently received the Academic Exhibitioner award for consistently high attainment. My study of Spanish has been particularly enjoyable and I intend to continue my interest in Hispanic culture and language at university. With this in mind I will make use of the opportunity to spend a year of my degree in Spain where I will benefit from full immersion in the language. I regularly contribute Spanish articles on a variety of topics to the school's Modern Languages magazine which is useful practice in writing Spanish in a variety of styles. Further to this, I obtained 100% in the Writing component of my Spanish AS level exam. Chemistry A level has taught me to follow a systematic and organised approach and from group research I have come to appreciate the importance of every member making a positive contribution to the team. Economics has given me a broad understanding of the business and financial worlds and I have enjoyed applying theories to real life situations. This was especially the case when taking part in the National Stock Market Competition, 'investing' a fictitious £100,000 in businesses and monitoring their progress over three months.

To learn more about the possible career options open to a Law graduate, I shadowed one of the partners at Hunt and Coombs solicitors. I was able to observe the daily work of a solicitor and played a part in assimilating information for his cases. Routine tasks such as filing law reports and books gave me a useful insight into the vast range of cases a solicitor may be involved in. In further preparation for my degree I am about to embark on an Open University module, 'An Introduction to Law'. This will allow me to familiarise myself with some of the relevant terms, theories and literature and provide me with a basic overview of the legal system before I start my degree. As I will be studying this alongside my schoolwork and other activities, it will also provide a good lesson in effective time management and prioritising of workload. As an active member of the school Law Society I take part in frequent debates, presentations and mock trials, which has helped to confirm my choice of degree.

Outside of school I enjoy my participation in the Combined Cadet Force. Having progressed to Lance Corporal, I now have responsibility for a platoon of younger Cadets. Complementing my role as a House Prefect, in which I supervise a younger year group and assist the staff with the smooth running of the school, this has developed in me strong leadership qualities and excellent oral communication. A range of exhilarating activities has furthered my confident approach to life. In kayaking and orienteering I have enjoyed seeing the landscape from a new perspective, as well as the competitive aspects of these sports. As a qualified lifeguard I have learnt specialist knowledge which, along with my First Aid certificate, should provide useful throughout my life. I have also gained a BTEC First Diploma in Public Services which has provided a stimulating contrast to my A level subjects.

In the long term I intend to qualify as a solicitor and work in a City law firm and, to utilise my Spanish skills, I am considering specialising in International Law. As a strongly dedicated student, with a variety of academic and extra-curricular interests, I feel that I have the qualities and motivation required to succeed in both my degree and my future career.

Management

Example 54

The world of business has an impact on every aspect of modern life, from people working in their own or someone else's company, to the products and services available to us as consumers. Having thoroughly enjoyed studying all aspects of this industry at college, I now wish to develop my understanding of Business Management at degree level.

During my AVCE Business I have enjoyed the vocational focus, enabling me to learn about the application of different aspects of business theory to practical situations. Through this course I have developed the ability to recognise and evaluate the ways in which a business can operate effectively, how to trade and sell efficiently, and the importance of good management. The components focusing on the legal framework of business practices and the health and safety aspects particularly interested me and I am keen to expand my knowledge of this area during my degree. The more hands-on elements of the AVCE, such as putting together a seven-day budget plan for a university student whilst studying business finance, have been an enjoyable way to learn. It is the crucial role good business management plays in everyday life which particularly appeals to me about this subject. At university I am looking forward to increasing my skill at distinguishing different management types and the effects these can have on the performance of the business. I am also excited at the prospect of learning about business' contribution to a country's wider economy and the effects of changing government policies.

Two weeks' work experience at the Immigration Service has supplemented my appreciation of Management, as I was able to observe the different routes into the UK labour market from the EU and the rest of the world. This placement also gave me the opportunity to utilise my language and interpersonal skills as effective communication with customers of all ages and backgrounds was necessary. Working in various retail outlets has allowed me to develop excellent customer service skills and to appreciate the impact of good management techniques on the shop floor. Whilst working for a linen company in a department store I was given sole responsibility for the day-to-day running of the shop. My approach involved setting myself daily retail targets and using my exceptional interpersonal skills to ensure I met them. At the moment I work in a busy duty free shop within an airport, updating stock and serving customers. As a till leader within my team I have developed my leadership qualities as well as learning how to work well in a large and busy team. As part of my college course I also completed a week's placement in a local pharmacy, implementing the skills I had gained during my previous employment experience. I look forward to making the most of the year in industry placement during my degree, gaining a broad insight into the industry and a real-life context to my studies.

At college I have been trained as a Mentor and Peer Buddy in order to help younger students with literacy and academic difficulties as well as personal issues such as bullying. This role has developed my confidence and maturity and I have appreciated the chance to contribute to the school community. In leisure time I like to unwind by cooking food from different regions, jogging and playing tennis. In the future I envisage myself in a management role and I intend to make use of every opportunity available at university in order to assist me in achieving this goal.

Example 55

An understanding of the principles behind effective business management is crucial to success in any sector of industry and requires knowledge of such diverse subject areas as psychology, accounting, marketing, law and Human Resources. By studying a Management degree I hope to develop specialist expertise in each of these areas, equipping myself with the skills in decision making, problem solving and critical evaluation of data required for a successful career in business.

At school I found Physics and Mathematics particularly fascinating subjects as they helped me to develop my ability to logically and methodically analyse information and to assess different approaches to solving problems. Studying Maths has ensured I have a strong grounding in the basic knowledge required for the quantitative aspects of Business Management and I have enjoyed the process of applying theoretical understanding gained in Pure Maths to real life situations in Physics. At present I am completing a Foundation year in Art and Design, a rewarding experience which has allowed me to utilise and explore my creativity and artistic flair. Although I have enjoyed my Art and Design course it has also highlighted that the most appropriate career for me will be one through which I can make a concrete contribution to society.

In reading Management in the UK I hope to take advantage of the benefits inherent in gaining a world-renowned qualification and being located close to the heart of the international business community. Studying in English will also give me daily opportunities to improve my skills in both academic and conversational English, preparing me well for my future career. In particular, I am looking forward to studying Management Science, gaining a detailed understanding of the theories and principles behind different approaches to managing people, resources and budgets. I am also keen to study topics such as Accounting and Finance, which are fundamental aspects of running a successful company of any size. The prospect of implementing the theories I will have studied within real life case studies also appeals to me, and I look forward to class discussions in which I can contribute my own opinions and learn from those of others.

Participating in the Young Enterprise scheme, acting as Operations Director for our team, has given me a very valuable insight into the leadership, communication skills and technical knowledge required to develop a successful business. Creating our business plan as a group required us to take account of everyone's views and to reach a consensus before progressing, testing our skills of interpersonal co-operation. The process of following the company's expansion highlighted the challenges a new business may face at different stages following its start up and my own responsibilities were to arrange production workshops, train other members of the company, source materials, implement plans and bring ideas to fruition. I have also completed work experience in an architecture firm and held a part-time job as a sales assistant, giving me experience of a range of employment environments and helping to determine my choice of degree. Completing my Duke of Edinburgh Award allowed me to work on my communication and teamwork skills, abilities that were well utilised during my voluntary placements in a charity shop and at a residential home for the elderly. In leisure time I enjoy keeping fit through playing basketball, tennis and badminton and I find my involvement in photography, drawing and ceramics helps me to relax.

In conclusion, as an energetic and proactive student, who is always willing to tackle new challenges, I look forward to making the most of the extensive opportuniuies for academic and personal development available at university.

Maths

Example 56

Ever since my father introduced me to the most basic concepts of Maths from an early age, Maths has been my favourite school subject. The advantage of such an early start has meant that I have been able to develop my own interest in the subject away from the classroom, making Maths in school significantly easier. I particularly enjoy the challenge of problem solving, taking great satisfaction upon arriving at the correct answer. Although I now undertake most of my study of Maths in school, I also spend a certain proportion of my own leisure time examining mathematical problems from websites as well as the booklet 'Advanced Problems in Mathematics' by Dr S.T.C. Siklos.

With the advance of science and technology, the importance and relevance that mathematical techniques have in everyday life has become more and more obvious. I believe that further enhancement of my knowledge in this subject would allow me to be more successful in my future career. I believe that I am well equipped to follow this programme, as I am currently studying A level Maths and AS level Further Maths, as well as taking modules in Pure Maths, Statistics, and Mechanics. I consider the course to be particularly suitable as the extra year gives me the opportunity to study Mathematics with a greater level of specialisation, which is ideal should I choose to pursue a career as a professional mathematician. I am confident that the versatility of a Maths degree will allow me to widen the scope of possible future career paths instead of restricting me to just one. The 'Master of Mathematics' choice also allows me to tailor the programme to suit my personal area of interest, which is statistics.

By attending some of the Maths taster courses held on offer by a University Summer Schools programme, I became certain that I would like to pursue a career in the field of maths; perhaps as a professional mathematician or as an accountant. The two taster courses I attended, ('Exploring Mathematics', a two day event held at Royal

Holloway and 'Women in Mathematics' held at UCL) not only allowed me to gain a greater sense of independence but also shows my commitment to the subject.

Apart from my dedication to mathematics, I have shown commitment to my studies by attending Cantonese lessons on a weekly basis at a Chinese School in Central London from the age of four. In a previous summer job, not only did I gain a greater understanding and insight into the herbal medicinal trade, but I also learnt the basics of conversational Mainland Chinese. Outside of the family, I have put my Cantonese lingual skills to practice on holidays to Hong Kong as well as during my part time work as a waitress. The varied nature of my previous paid employment has given me a wider view of different vocations as well as helping to sustain my self-sufficiency. Both my summer spent at a telemarketing company and my role as an active member of the Sixth Form Council have made me more confident in expressing my opinions, and enhanced my listening skills.

I am confident that I would make an excellent addition to your institution, both academically and socially, and will relish the challenges and opportunities that university life will undoubtedly bring.

Example 57

An understanding of Maths and the proofs it can provide is a core aspect of many key industries, including science, engineering, technology and business. The scope of its applications and its fundamental role in evaluating, defining and developing these sectors of the economy fascinates me, particularly the increasing importance of Statistics within banking and finance. As this is the area in which I hope to pursue my future career, I am confident I will benefit greatly from the rigorous academic challenge of a Maths degree.

At school I have taken a thoughtful and diligent approach to my studies and have found Maths and Physics, to a large extent definable as a highly developed area of applied Maths, particularly interesting. My background growing up in a poverty-stricken area of China has been significant in this fascination as I observed the impact of poor access to technological development on a daily basis. This has given me a genuine and heartfelt appreciation of the profound importance of mathematical knowledge in ensuring the continuation of advances in science that can positively impact all our lives. Studying modules of my Maths and Further Maths AS levels independently has tested my initiative and commitment to the subject, and ensured that I am familiar with directing my own learning. Pure Maths, especially calculus and trigonometry, has been one of my favourite areas as it necessitates a high degree of proof whilst underpinning all other aspects of the wider subject area. The extensive scope of Applied Maths also intrigues me and I am keen to develop my knowledge of the relevance of Statistics to areas such as investment banking, risk management and computational science. During my degree I hope to develop skills in reasoning, logic and analysis through focusing on thought processes and problem solving techniques. Having benefited from completing my further education in the UK, I thrive in a high achieving environment and I hope to take advantage of the opportunity to remain in the UK in order to study at some of the best universities in the world, particularly for the field of Maths.

Spending a month working for an industrial company has given me an insight into the working environment and an understanding of how mathematical concepts can be usefully applied in a range of business situations. The placement also allowed me to take responsibility for individual tasks, developing my independence and confidence in my abilities. At school in China, I enjoyed contributing to the student community as a class monitor and I hope to involve myself similarly in university life through societies and voluntary work. As a maths assistant, helping the teacher to motivate the class and ensuring students understood the concepts involved, I also enhanced my leadership and communication skills. Representing my school at table tennis in China has given me useful experience of working towards effective and supportive teamwork. In leisure time I enjoy swimming and horse riding for both relaxation and exercise and I hope to continue my involvement in both of these hobbies. Participation in chess has helped to develop my cognitive and decision-making skills and I also enjoy exploring my creativity and imaginative flair through practising Chinese painting.

As a hardworking, considered and outgoing student I am looking forward to significantly advancing my understanding of Maths and its uses in the world and I intend to make full use of the opportunities available to me at university.

Example 58

After completing an Access to Higher Education course with the original intention of pursuing a career in radiography, I have come to the conclusion that the most appropriate degree for me is one which allows me to explore my interest and talent for Mathematics and its applications in greater detail.

Whilst studying my Access course I found the components which appealed to me most were those with a high mathematical content. Studying several credits of Maths, combined with my Maths A level, has given me a solid grounding in the basics of the subject. Meanwhile, the Physics and Biology modules have given me a fascinating insight into the role of Maths in science and industry, from medical advances to engineering innovations. Throughout my Access course I have worked hard to develop and refine effective study skills and have brought a patient and logical approach to my studies. In particular I have found great satisfaction in analysing and evaluating data in order to solve practical problems and my attention to detail has allowed me to achieve a high standard of academic work throughout this course. After thoroughly researching my options on completion of the Access programme, I am confident that a career using my mathematical skills will be suitably rewarding and will offer me the academic challenge I am looking for. Although I am excited by the prospect of studying all aspects of the subject, techniques such as advanced calculus and its applications and the use of different forms of algebra in encryption and coding systems fascinate me especially. The relationship between Maths and computing is a further interest of mine and I am looking forward to understanding the use of statistical and mathematical modelling in data analysis programs.

My employment history has also equipped me with a range of skills transferable to degree level study. Utilising my fluency in French, English and Arabic, I have worked as a translator. Much of this work involved interpreting in French and English for solicitors and their clients and translating relevant legal documents. I enjoyed playing a part in helping all members of the community to access the legal system and developed my ability to work accurately and with attention to detail, to manage time and resources efficiently and to meet regular deadlines. My job required me to meet and work with members of the public from a diversity of backgrounds, ensuring I have a high level of interpersonal and communication skills.

Becoming a father five months ago has also played a significant role in my personal growth. The increased responsibility and new level of maturity associated with this has been a principal motivator in my decision to follow a career in a subject I have a passion for. Although I am confident a Maths degree will open up a range of options for me I am most interested in becoming a teacher, as I feel helping children to understand and appreciate the role of Maths in the world around them will be very rewarding. As a mature applicant I have investigated my possible career paths fully and I am looking forward to returning to university and tackling the challenges of an undergraduate degree.

Media Studies

Example 59

Through studying Media I hope to gain a theoretical foundation in the main schools of thought as well as extensive practical skills in media production which will be useful experience for my intended career in the digital media industry. I am also interested in understanding the internal structure of the major institutions of both mass and elite media and how they relate to power, authority and the general population.

Whilst studying Media at A level I have enjoyed learning technical codes, lighting focus and the contrast between connotation and denotation, and particularly the impact new computer technologies can have on these areas. In conjunction with AS level IT this has motivated me to focus my degree studies on new media and the role of digital technology. I look forward to gaining a deeper understanding of technical issues such as broadcast convergence technologies and the rapidly growing industry of interactive services, which I believe will be a key feature of even the most mainstream media within under five years. The speed of developments within the last few years is inspiring and I am excited about the future direction of this industry, and my own possible role within it.

In order to understand the media industry more fully I did my Year 10 work placement at the Yorkshire Television Studios, working in the Production department. Inspired by this I applied for several of the BBC's work experience placements and was lucky enough to be accepted for a fascinating two-week placement at BBC Asian Interactive, a digital multi-media channel. During my placement I worked on programme content, helped research a programme about South Indian music and was involved in the coverage of the Nottingham Mela. As well as practical experience of digital production, researching and presenting I benefited from working as part of a very busy team under pressure to meet strict deadlines.

As a College Student Representative I have been responsible for liaising between staff and students, and was involved last year in a successful campaign to improve provision of extra-curricular clubs at lunchtimes. My two years in the Army Cadets, rising to the rank of Junior Officer, featured a continual emphasis on teamwork, leadership, discipline and focus. These skills were utilised on my Silver Duke of Edinburgh expedition in Bavaria, and I also developed my interpersonal skills working closely with others in the team, practised my AS German, and acquired new skills such as map reading. In my leisure time I enjoy travelling around the region playing bass guitar in my band as well as taking part in volleyball, rowing and hockey clubs. At university I intend to continue to participate in sports as well as making use of music practice facilities and perhaps forming another band.

In the future I intend to stay at university for postgraduate training and I believe this broad based degree will provide me with useful experience of the relevant theoretical concepts, critical evaluation and practical innovations. I am a hardworking and highly motivated student and I look forward to meeting the challenges of university life.

Example 60

The media industry is central to modern life, channelling information, education, politics, art and entertainment. My studies of Media at A level first interested me in this topic, and I particularly enjoyed my coursework exploring the semiotics of television advertising. At university I hope to learn to develop a critical approach to modern media and an understanding of both its history and its possible future.

My interest in working in and studying this industry has been enhanced by attendance at a BBC Media Careers Information Day which gave me a better understanding of the requirements of different jobs, and by a two-work experience placement at my local music radio station. This placement involved shadowing a radio presenter and several production staff and I learnt a range of technical skills particularly regarding digital media production. I also had the opportunity to discuss possible career paths with those already working in this field and I found this very informative. Above all I was advised to gain as much practical experience as possible, which I intend to continue to do during my time at university.

Studying Philosophy A level has helped me to develop a reasoned and logical approach to argument, and I have enjoyed the regular opportunities for debates in class. Philosophy has also introduced me to some of the principal schools of critical thought which I feel will be useful background when studying the different theoretical approaches to media analysis. I am particularly excited about the prospect of understanding how topics such as aesthetics and ethics relate to the media. Studying the growth of democracy in the UK and how different social groups have contributed to this has interested me in the transformations brought about by industrial capitalism and how the media's role differs between developing and developed nations. The context of globalisation and the experiences of migrants and migrancy is another fascinating aspect of this which I hope to pursue further. At college I have always felt the benefits of group research and I look forward to the opportunity to discuss these issues with tutors and my fellow students.

Writing for the college's monthly magazine has given me some experience of print journalism and refined my written communication skills. My articles are usually focused on finding a local element or school analogy for major global issues such as immigration and asylum seeking. I enjoy reading several journals and magazines on these issues and I particularly aspire towards the style of accessible but hard-hitting reporting practised by 'New Internationalist'. As there was a lack of extra-curricular activities available at college which interested me I set up and now organise a creative writing club which meets weekly and allows students to read their work aloud and accept constructive criticism.

In my leisure time I enjoy training for my position as captain of my local hockey club, as well as adventure sports such as snow boarding and paragliding. At university I hope to continue to practise these sports and to be involved in founding or running relevant clubs. In the long term I envisage myself eventually working as a newspaper or magazine journalist covering issues of global injustice. In order to succeed in this field I will need a range of experiences and skills and I feel my degree and extra-curricular activities at university will be the first step towards reaching my goals.

Medicine

Example 61

Medicine appeals to me as a way to use both science and compassion to help people through treatment, advice and reassurance. In my job as a Healthcare Assistant I have found there is a limit to the help I can give. In qualifying as a doctor I will have the knowledge and skill to provide a much higher level of care.

Having previously begun an Accountancy degree at university in Brazil I have experience of tertiary level study. Despite pressure from my family I found this was not the right career for me, but I enjoyed the opportunities to explore topics at a much higher level, to carry out independent research and learn from others in presentation groups. After this I left Brazil for the UK and began working towards my goal of becoming a doctor. Supplementing my school studies, I look forward to learning about the functions of the body, the basis for all further medical study. In particular I am interested in Palliative care as it relates to Oncology as I feel the doctor's role in supporting cancer patients and their family through potential bereavement is extremely important. The issues of psychiatry and ethics are also fascinating to me, empathising with people with mental health problems and respecting patients' beliefs.

As a Healthcare Assistant I have enjoyed the high level of patient interaction and have been able to develop strong relationships with some, learning about their diagnoses and treatments. Working in a team alongside a range of healthcare professionals I have learnt about the demands and rewards of being a doctor. More than anything I have seen the importance of keeping patients informed about their treatment and condition, dealing compassionately with relatives, and communicating effectively with others on the medical team. My work has given me practical skills in manual handling, personal care, and measuring and recording details such as pulse rate and temperature. I now wish to increase my knowledge to a much higher level by studying Medicine. In a previous job as an administration assistant at a psychiatric hospital I typed transcripts of patient consultations. This allowed me to learn something of the range and characteristics of mental health problems as well as highlighting the need for confidentiality.

My sense of fulfilment in helping people has led me to take part in support groups for people with weight problems. I was once overweight myself and I have been pleased to be able to support and encourage others through discussing my own experiences. This improved my own confidence, as I became familiar with communicating with new people of all ages and backgrounds. I feel that my upbringing in total poverty in Brazil has been formative in my personal development. At the age of nine I began to help my mother with the housework and to work in my parents' shop. As a result I am a responsible and determined person who is willing to work extremely hard. As a student and as an employee I have worked well under pressure. I also recognise my own limitations and am not afraid to ask for assistance when necessary. In times of stress I use my hobby of regular swimming to unwind and I also enjoy reading about different world cultures.

In the long term I hope to become a surgeon specialising in colorectal procedures. I am a well-motivated and hard working person and fully committed to becoming a doctor. I intend to make the most of every opportunity available at university and I feel that I have the skills and dedication to make a positive contribution to society through medicine.

Example 62

My interest in Medicine began on a visit to India, during which I witnessed the disabilities and deaths that result from preventable diseases such as cholera and malaria. My own cousin suffers from severe sensory neural hearing loss as a result of his mother contracting rubella during her first trimester. The fact that in the UK this could have been prevented by a routine vaccination is a stark illustration of the remarkable impact the medical profession has. I have a passion for science, and for its potential to contribute positively to people's lives. At school I have thoroughly enjoyed my Chemistry A level, particularly the group research and practical experiments, and I found learning about human anatomy and physiology in Biology very interesting. I am looking forward to studying clinical procedures at university and acquiring sufficient knowledge to give accurate diagnoses and prescriptions. I am passionate about raising awareness of health issues and am currently setting up diabetes awareness sessions at local supermarkets. I also work with UK Transplant to raise awareness of donor cards amongst the Asian community.

During work experience in a postnatal unit I assisted the midwifery team in the care of the babies, and observed premature babies being cared for in incubators. Contributing to staff meetings in which patients' progress was discussed, I learnt about a variety of issues affecting the hospital. Recently I completed a clinical attachment at a hospital with a consultant Audiological Physician, a fascinating experience from which I learnt a great deal. Attending multidisciplinary meetings I noticed how professionals from different specialties came together to form a team to give the best possible care. I also attended a clinic for babies and children undergoing chemotherapy for life threatening cancers. This gave me some appreciation of working in a sensitive atmosphere with terminally ill children and distraught parents, requiring a tactful and compassionate manner.

For the past 18 months I have worked part time at a home for people with severe learning and physical disabilities. This has been extremely rewarding working in a team of carers to deliver all aspects of personal care, including manual handling using hoists and administration of daily drugs. On night shifts I have the responsibility of being shift leader, requiring me to show leadership, initiative and a calm but efficient response to any problems. I use good verbal communication to ensure the staff work together and to give a precise verbal handover at the end of a shift. Monitoring residents to ensure the correct drugs and tests are given has required attention to detail, and through maintaining accurate reports I have developed clear written communication and good organisation.

In my year out I will be working with children and disabled adults in the UK as well as travelling to Costa Rica. As school Charity Rep I am involved in fundraising events for breast cancer and heart disease charities. I enjoy sports and captained the athletics team for several years, organising events and supporting team members. I also enjoy performing on stage and recently played the lead role in a school production. My participation on the Public Speaking team has boosted my confidence in presenting and justifying my views and I also enjoy working on the team which produces the college newsletter.

In the long term I hope to specialise in Dermatology and to be able to deliver the best possible healthcare to the community. I am totally committed to becoming a doctor and I feel that I have the skills and motivation to succeed at university and in my future career.

Midwifery

Example 63

Since completing a work experience placement shadowing a community-based midwife for three weeks and finding the role to be varied, stimulating and rewarding, I have had an ambition to study Midwifery at university.

At school I have found Biology A level a particularly interesting subject as I am fascinated by the anatomy and physiology of the human body. Practical classes have always been my favourite as I enjoy learning from hands-on experience. As such I have found experiments in Biology and Chemistry, such as making aspirin and studying the growth of different bacteria, very exciting. English A level has been an opportunity to develop a different approach to study, and I have especially enjoyed the insight into other cultures which our range of literature has given me. Having studied both Science and Arts subjects at A level I have strong communication skills and a logical approach to problem solving. I have enjoyed opportunities to work in pairs and groups as I find it beneficial to discuss issues with others.

During my time at university I am looking forward to the range of disciplines which are covered in Midwifery, and to the blocks of practical experience which will allow me to practise clinical skills before starting my career. As well as the biological aspects and technical skills required of a midwife, I am looking forward to studying peripheral areas such as the emotional health of the mother during pregnancy and the requirements of mothers with special needs and disabilities. My work experience placement introduced me to many aspects of the midwife's role and I look forward to putting this in an academic context. In particular, the importance of effective communication skills with both patients and the many other healthcare professionals the midwives interacted with was demonstrated. For the last year I have worked at the weekends and during school holidays as a care assistant at a nursing home, talking to patients and helping the nurses to handle the patients and administer medicines. This has given me an appreciation of some of the different careers available in healthcare, as well as experience of interacting in an empathetic and sensitive manner with patients and of working within a team of assistants.

From the age of five I have spent much of my leisure time training and performing in ballet and modern dance, and have competed many times at national level, most recently winning the silver medal at the British Under-18s Dance finals. As a dancer I am responsible for managing myself as a performer, ensuring I maintain my fitness levels, devising my timetable and meeting potential agents and employees. This has given me skills in self-motivation, discipline and time management. Dancing remains an important part of my life and I hope to continue performing at university, setting up or running dance clubs and organising performances. I have performed in the West End, toured Austria and Italy, and have also coached children up to the age of 12 voluntarily at a ballet school. I am a motivated and disciplined student with a range of active interests and a strong commitment to working as a midwife. This degree will equip me well for my future career and I feel I have the qualities to be able to make the most of the opportunities available to me at university.

Example 64

As a future midwife, I look forward to working as part of a

multi-disciplinary team of health professionals providing care for women and babies at such a significant, and potentially stressful, time in their lives. Having witnessed a close relative suffer several complications during pregnancy and labour I am well aware of the impact a good midwife can have on the health and well being of a mother and her family. At university I am looking forward to learning about the processes of a normal, healthy pregnancy and gaining the clinical skills to recognise deviations from this and to know how to treat the problem. Having studied Sociology A level as well as Sciences, the wider sociological factors which can help to ensure a problem free pregnancy, and how these can be made accessible to everyone, is of particular interest to me. In my free time I enjoy following medical developments in relevant journals such as New Scientist, Nature and Midwifery Today. Recently I have been particularly interested in the debate regarding the proposed changes to midwifery practice which will give expectant mothers increased choice, and the wider legal and ethical impact of these. Further to this I look forward to future study of the midwife's role within the health service, common ethical dilemmas, and the ethical implications of an individual midwife's actions.

Whilst completing my A levels part-time I have also been working as a healthcare assistant in a maternity ward, and have recently completed the NVQ training to become a maternity care assistant. I have found the training course fascinating, learning about childbirth and the needs of parents and babies, and it has confirmed my desire to continue training in this area. Studying the wider needs of women patients, including contraception and prevention of STIs, has been especially interesting and I am keen to take the specialist option in HIV studies during my degree. My work at the hospital has allowed me to observe in detail the midwives at work, and to make my own contribution to improving the women's experience whilst on the ward through providing help, support and advice, for example with regard to breastfeeding and postnatal care.

Through taking a gap year I hope to broaden my experience of different cultures and languages, and will be funding my own travels. Using my organisational and planning abilities I have arranged a round the world trip which will include three months volunteering at a Red Cross orphanage in Japan and one month teaching at a school in Kenya. I will be working full-time as a maternity care assistant until March and on returning from my travels, I will be volunteering as a carer in the UK with CSV. As well as being an exciting experience I hope it will help to improve my confidence, interpersonal skills and independence during my year out, which will be useful on starting at university.

At school I enjoy playing on the basketball, rugby and chess teams. Using my leadership skills I also set up and now manage a basketball club for Lower School children. As part of my school's volunteering programme I have spent three months mentoring primary school children in English and Maths. This has been a rewarding way to contribute to the community and has taught me valuable communicative and interpersonal techniques. I also enjoy taking part in extreme sports such as wakeboarding and surfing whenever I can. As a highly motivated and well-rounded individual I intend to make a positive contribution to university life and look forward to facing the challenges of higher education.

Music

Example 65

In applying to study Music I am looking forward to combining a wide range of subjects from Politics to Maths in the understanding of the development and function of music in human society. Music has been used for millennia to express ideas and emotions and can be used as a vehicle through which to engage with different cultures. Studying these subjects, as well as technical and performance skills, will equip me well for a range of careers by enabling me to develop abilities of critical analysis, coherent expression and communication skills in a range of media.

Playing the piano since the age of five has allowed me to achieve a high standard in performance and in tutoring others. I have passed the teaching diploma, and enjoy having the opportunity to inspire others with a love of music. I also find that verbally explaining different techniques to my pupils has enhanced my own understanding of the underlying principles of musicology which performance alone has not required me to consider. On the saxophone I am currently working toward Grade 8 and I particularly enjoy the diversity of the music which I typically perform with these instruments. As well as playing with the Jazz Band, and my own rock band outside school, I frequently accompany scenes in school plays on the piano.

Studying Maths and Computing at school has stimulated my interest in the relationship between both these subjects and Music and I am keen to explore this area further at university. Maths has developed in me useful skills of analysis and application of modelling which can be transferred to music and I am fascinated by the function of maths in composition, often without the composer's explicit understanding of this. I hope to progress in my understanding of mathematical modelling in music and to have the facilities to analyse this further. In Computing A level I have particularly enjoyed combining practical and technical skills and, having read up about this topic. I am interested in studying the use of compositional mapping of mathematical spaces in experimental music. As a future music professional I am also interested in the recent impact of technological advances on the commercial music industry.

As a Millennium Volunteer I have so far completed over 100 hours of community service, leading a music performance group at an Age Concern day centre. This has developed my interpersonal skills to a high level as I work with volunteers of all ages, elderly visitors and their carers, and the staff at the centre. Leading the group requires me to plan and deliver each weekly session as well as giving me confidence in performance and presentations. Each session involves a brief introduction to a specific area of music, and ongoing practice of a choral movement to be performed at the Christmas party. Although many of the singers are talented and take rehearsals very seriously, the emphasis is on enjoyment and staying active and I have been moved by the impact that involvement in music can have on a person's quality of life.

In my free time I enjoy gymnastics lessons, and at university I intend to set up a society for this activity, or get involved in the committee if one already exists. I also plan to make the most of all the opportunities to be involved in music groups, and perhaps to set up another rock band. As an active and committed student I believe that I will be a positive asset to the university and look forward to contributing fully to the course.

Example 66

Understanding and appreciating music has been important to me since first playing the drums with the Youth Band at my Youth Club six years ago. This was my first participation in music and I found the intensity of rehearsals followed by the thrill of performing to be exhilarating. Since then I have taken every opportunity to widen my experience of live performance as well as studying academic aspects of the subject at school and in college.

Studying for my BTEC Diploma in Popular Music widened my awareness of different genres as well as giving me the tools with which to analyse my own and other people's compositions. In particular it has introduced me to the basics of computer composition and music technology; an area I wish to specialise in at university. Supplementing my IT GCSE I have been fascinated to learn how to use software packages such as ProTools and Logic Audio Pro in music production. At university I hope to increase my understanding of the technical principles behind this as well as to have the opportunity to debate the possible impact of future developments in hardware and software. I believe that hardware technology will play a part in every aspect of the future music industry, and I am excited about using the recording and mixing studios, practising the use of software for recording and sequencing, and gaining a deeper understanding of the mechanics and scope of digital sound design.

As well as continuing to play drums and percussion in the Youth Band, I have recently become involved in a local youth radio station as a DJ. This has given me a new perspective of what it means to be a music professional and I believe the technical skills I will gain at university will be invaluable to my development in this area. Our Youth Band is becoming well known locally, having played in several recent festivals celebrating urban music. My involvement in this has given me skills in teamwork and co-operation, which are essential in ensuring all members of the band are performing at their best.

At the Youth Club I also volunteer as a mentor. This involves advising and supporting younger members of the community and I believe it plays an important role in helping children to develop their potential. It has been a significant part of my personal development as I have enjoyed the responsibility of the role and I am now involved in training new members of the mentoring team. This experience has inspired me to increase my volunteering and I intend to get involved in similar projects at university or in my new local area. As a hobby I enjoy drawing and painting, particularly abstract pictures in the style of Mark Rothko, as I enjoy experimenting with combinations of colours and seeing people's different reactions to my results.

In the future I envisage myself working in the music industry either as a DJ promoting urban and experimental music or in a coaching role, encouraging young people to express themselves through music. I believe that music plays a part in everybody's life and will provide an exciting, stimulating and constantly evolving career.

Nursing

Example 67

Since completing my work experience in a hospice for people with a terminal illness, I have been committed to pursuing a career in Nursing. My A level Biology has provided me with a background in the science of the human body and I have enjoyed learning about the functions and interactions of the different systems. My coursework investigating the functions of proteins on plants and animals has been very interesting and has allowed me to develop my research skills. In Chemistry I have again found the practical work very engaging, especially the challenge of collating everyone's results to draw a conclusion during group research.

Three weeks of work experience at a hospice was very influential in my decision to apply for Nursing and taught me the daily reality of caring for people who may be distressed, uncomfortable and frightened. During my time there one of the elderly residents died, which was upsetting for me but I felt inspired by the professional yet compassionate manner with which the staff dealt with the lady in question and with her grieving family. To confirm my suitability for Nursing I have since obtained a part-time job as a Ward Assistant in a busy general hospital. This has given me the opportunity to work within the ward team ensuring our section is run smoothly and our patients can receive the best possible care. This job has taught me a great deal about the importance of hygiene as well as the roles of the different professionals and how they interact. During night shifts I am the Supervisor, with responsibility for ensuring all the Ward Assistants' duties are completed according to the schedule and writing a concise shift report for the handover at the end of the shift. These extra duties have allowed me to develop my interpersonal and leadership skills and increased my confidence when dealing with colleagues and the public.

Working in a hospital and observing treatments being administered around me has captured my curiosity and I am very excited about learning all aspects of Nursing *during my degree. In particular, I have an interest in public health, which has received a great deal of press recently due to the problems with MRSA, and how to best manage care and treatment within complex multiple environments. Related topics such as healthcare law and ethics also interest me and I enjoy following such issues in the broadsheet newspapers. The clinical placements, with the opportunity to implement and enhance my interpersonal skills, will be excellent practice for the working environment and I also look forward to the opportunity to debate subjects with other students across the healthcare programmes.*

As a Senior Prefect at school I have been responsible for organising a team of eight Prefects and assisting the staff in the smooth running of the school. This has further developed my leadership qualities and I enjoy making a responsible contribution to the school. For the last five years I have competed at national level in water skiing representing my region, first in the Junior section, and now in the Adult competitions. Competing at this level requires frequent training and a great deal of self-discipline in order to improve my ability. This year I have been selected for the national team and will be competing at the World Championships in Tokyo, where I hope to be placed at least third. I also enjoy other water sports such as wind surfing and sailing and I intend to be involved in adventure sports societies at university. I am a highly motivated student with interests in many areas and a genuine commitment to a career as a nurse and I look forward to making the most of the opportunities available to me at university.

Example 68

In training to be a nurse, I hope to put my compassionate manner and enjoyment of working with others to good use, helping to alleviate patients' suffering. Having worked as a Ward Clerk for several years, I have an appreciation of what the job entails and the requirements of a good nurse. For the past two years I have studied a part-time Access Course to prepare myself academically for my degree and I now wish to take the next step on my new career path by taking a Nursing degree.

Working as a Ward Clerk has been a useful introduction to the hospital environment. In my day-to-day work I deal with patients, visitors, health and social care workers, executives and support staff with a friendly and professional manner and have learned about the different roles of these people. As I am based in neonatal Intensive Care, my job includes updating the patient information records each morning, organising medication requests from the pharmacy, assisting parents who are staying on-site, answering phone calls, booking appointments and organising the repair and maintenance of the ward facilities. This work has given me inside knowledge of how an NHS Trust is run and has shown me the difficult aspects of Nursing, such as dealing with the deaths of babies and supporting grieving families. Using the hospital computer system as an integral part of my job has developed in me confident ICT skills which I will be able to make use of both during my degree and in my future work. As a Ward Clerk I do my best to make people's experience of hospital less stressful but I look forward to being able to make a real difference to patients' quality of treatment as a nurse.

During my Access Course I have especially enjoyed the modules on Science and Prevention of Infection as these have allowed me to make use of my employment background to add context to the theory. Communications has also been an interesting part of the course and I feel skill in this area is one of the most important qualities in a good nurse. At university I hope to build on my academic knowledge and learn how to put research into practice during clinical placements. At this stage I am planning to follow the Mental Health route and I am particularly interested in studying the sociological and psychological aspects of effective patient care.

In leisure time I enjoy my position on a local football team which is currently top of our league. Regular team training provides excellent exercise and I enjoy meeting players from all walks of life. As the club's social secretary I put my organisational skills to good use, arranging fundraising and team building events such as karaoke nights and pub quizzes. I also enjoy staying up-to-date with current issues in Nursing by reading journals such as the Nursing Times. Applying to study Nursing is a personal challenge for me and I hope to make the most of this opportunity to prove my academic ability and to improve my career prospects. I am embarking on a Nursing career with a realistic awareness of what it entails and I look forward to taking on its rewards and challenges.

Optometry

Example 69

My interest in studying Optometry was initially sparked by visits to a local practice, which introduced me to the fascinating role of the Optometrist in examining sight, looking for signs of disease, giving advice on eye health and prescribing and fitting glasses. In applying for this degree I hope to equip myself with the practical skills and technical knowledge to pursue a rewarding career within the healthcare sector, making use of my scientific ability and my interpersonal abilities to contribute to improving others' quality of life.

Visiting a local optometry practice gave me the opportunity to familiarise myself with the typical daily routine of an Optometrist and I was particularly interested in the high level of interaction with patients and the variety of work involved. Observing a laser surgery procedure, and my own experience of having glasses prescribed and fitted, has deepened my fascination with the subject of eye health and I have enjoyed enhancing my knowledge through relevant literature and television programmes. Conversations with professionals involved in healthcare have confirmed my commitment to this career path and have opened my eyes to the range of environments in which an Optometrist may be employed. As someone who enjoys applying science to a hands-on and practical situation I feel confident I will be well suited to this type of work.

Having already studied the first year of a Podiatry degree, I am aware of the academic standards expected at university level and familiar with using effective time management to meet the demands of a degree course. Although I enjoyed many aspects of my previous degree studies, particularly the opportunity to undertake practical work in a hospital environment and the chance to help improve people's health and wellbeing, I did not find the subject especially inspiring. After visiting an optometry practice and researching the subject in my own time, I became committed to changing my degree course to one in which

I will feel truly motivated. At school I particularly enjoyed Physics, especially optics, and I am keen to study this aspect of Optometry at university and to understand fully the processes behind assessing a person's need for glasses and evaluating the most appropriate lenses. I am also eager to study the ways in which changing technology impacts on developments in the field and the possible innovations that may form part of my work in the future.

My hospital placement during my Podiatry degree provided me with a valuable opportunity to learn first hand about contributing to a multidisciplinary healthcare team, interacting sensitively and empathetically with patients and applying theoretical knowledge to real life situations. With responsibility for my own patients throughout their treatment until they were returned to the ward, I soon gained in confidence, leadership and communication skills. This was the most rewarding and challenging part of my Podiatry studies and I look forward to utilising my interpersonal skills during optometry placements. At present I am undertaking a year out, in order to fully prepare myself for embarking on my new degree course.

My goal for the future is to gain experience as an Optometrist in the UK, before broadening my horizons through contributing to the development of healthcare in developing countries. Ultimately I hope to return to Glasgow and set up my own practice in the area, and I am confident that this degree programme will equip me with the skills and knowledge to successfully embark on the path towards this ambition.

Example 70

Studying Optometry is the next step towards my aim of becoming a Registered Optometrist, increasing people's physical and emotional health through protecting and improving their sight. The multi-skilled environment, making use of scientific and interpersonal skills as well as practical ability, also appeals to me. I have enjoyed the gateway into understanding the human body provided by my Biology A level and I am now seeking greater intellectual stimulation. At university I look forward to learning to use advanced optical equipment, and how to provide the best possible care in the future. In particular I am excited at the prospect of hands-on training in clinical procedures, and the opportunity to increase my knowledge of anatomy and physiology, especially with regard to the eyes.

My interest was confirmed by working at an eye infirmary. Assisting the Optometrist, I researched the effects of new drugs on patients, administering tests in refraction, reading speed, low vision and contrast and sensitivity. This has given me some relevant practical skills and I enjoyed the high level of patient interaction. Working at an eye surgery I was able to see the range of tests an Optometrist performs, beyond the simple eye tests available on the high street. From discussions with the Optometrist I was able to learn about the possible career options and the activities involved. Whilst testing patients I implemented some of my A level theory as well as learning more about general eye health.

As Team Leader with the Combined Cadet Force I had responsibility for 16 cadets, training and guiding them through various skills tests and working with the Corporal to set their weekly goals. This has improved my leadership skills and communication with people of a range of ages. I have found when managing others that a willingness to prioritise and delegate tasks is important, as well as leading by example. The fact that all my Cadets passed the tests I helped them through was a boost to my confidence. Assisting teachers as a Biology Support Student I helped others to understand basic principles before applying these to more complex problems. In my community I am involved in helping older people to access services, which has required me to listen actively to their needs and discuss with others what help may be available. I am also involved in the care of my grandparents, booking appointments, helping them to understand things, and assisting with cleaning and other every day tasks. Both of these roles have given me great personal satisfaction.

Being captain of the school football team I motivate others and ensure that every member makes a full contribution. I am also Head Boy of Sports, encouraging and organising participation. My principal sport is Tae Kwon Do, in which I have won the World Championship Silver Medal, and Gold in the Freestyle Amsterdam Championship. Achieving this has required determination, persistence, and mental and physical agility. As training requires a lot of input I am adept at time management in order to balance my academic and sporting activities.

In the future I intend to run my own opticians, and eventually to become a professor of Optometry, passing on my enthusiasm to others. As a mentally and physically active student with a range of interests and skills, and a genuine passion for the subject, I hope to contribute positively to university life and make the most of the opportunities on offer.

Osteopathy

Example 71

Accompanying my grandmother on her visits to an Osteopath, and the inspiring conversations I had there sparked my initial interest in this career. Human physiology fascinates me and I am enthusiastic about working with a diverse range of people to support and sustain lives.

Shadowing a doctor has given me an understanding of the daily routine of a hospital and an appreciation of the stress placed on doctors. Observing him at work I saw that good communication and explaining procedures fully is essential in reassuring anxious patients and their families. At the Maxillofacial Surgery department I shadowed a surgeon and was impressed by the intricate surgery performed. Whilst I thoroughly enjoyed this experience, it made me realise that medicine, per say, is not the career for me. As I enjoy problem solving and research I am looking forward to resolving patient concerns by listening to the patient and applying my own knowledge. Volunteering at a centre for mentally disabled people I learnt to cope in distressing situations and to have an empathetic manner. My First Aid course gave me some basic medical knowledge and the ability to keep calm under pressure.

During my gap year I will be furthering my experience by working as a nursing assistant and I am looking forward to meeting new challenges. I will also work on a project with HIV affected street children in Mombasa. By assisting in health education I hope to be able to make a genuine difference to the lives of the children I will work with. This experience will increase my maturity, self-reliance and flexibility, as I will have to adapt to a new culture, language and standard of living.

At school I was part of a team organising a variety of fundraising activities for charity and I learnt to appreciate the value of cohesive teamwork in achieving our objectives efficiently. Fundraising has also been an important element of my work with a Leprosy charity. In the Young Enterprise programme I enjoyed discussing our options with my team and, as Director, collating these ideas into one plan. This improved my leadership and confidence in motivating others, and our team won an award for our efforts. These are skills which I feel will benefit me as an Osteopath.

Leading a healthy lifestyle is important to me and I am currently training to run the London Marathon. Training in all weathers requires motivation and resilience but I find focusing on sports as I am doing them helps me to unwind. I also play badminton competitively. I intend to be a proactive member of the university and look forward to continuing these activities and making many new friends. My 100% attendance at school has won me several awards and I will be bringing this committed attitude to my degree and subsequent career.

In the long term I would like to work in Partnership with a General Practice as I feel it would be rewarding to build strong relationships with patients throughout their lives. I am dedicated to becoming an Osteopath and I believe I have the skills and motivation required to succeed at university and in my future career.

Example 72

The opportunity to deliver first rate care and attention to those most in need of it has always been at the forefront of my career aspirations. Indeed, I have been interested in the care profession since I was a child, but due to financial hardship within my family and the social problems that this has caused, I failed to achieve the necessary qualifications at school. The birth of my last child who is asthmatic and suffers from severe eczema has precipitated my return to education in order to realise my ambition; it has been caring for him that reminded me of my childhood dream. The support of the hospital staff has made me more determined to achieve my goal.

In 2009, I decided to match my interest and ambition to my skills and enrol for the Pre-Access to Science Study. I am currently taking the Access to Science course to develop and improve my knowledge and skills in Biology, Chemistry, Mathematics, Psychology, English, IT, Study Skills, Professional Communication Skills, Welfare and Society. These will improve my chance of gaining admission to university, having not achieved the conventional qualifications necessary. Despite this, I believe this course has helped me to communicate effectively with various people; meeting deadlines and situations has, I feel, equipped me with the necessary skills needed to specialise in Osteopathy. I particularly enjoy Biology due to its close relationship with Osteopathy and the workings of the body.

As a mother of three, I enjoy working with my children and supporting them with their school assignments. I make a particular effort to work closely with their schools to improve their performance and progress. In addition, I worked voluntarily as a co-ordinator for the youth section of my church. My role involved organising, planning and co-ordinating programmes, collaborating with other youth clubs in the community, taking part in exhibitions, competitions, festivals and song revivals. I also fundraise for the local care home and Children in Need. These roles have improved my ability to think things through and solve problems.

I have had the good fortune to shadow an Osteopath at a local practice and was able to observe how understanding and promoting the correct mechanical structure and function of a patient can lead to an improvement in well being. I was able to talk with a number of Osteopaths about studying to enter the profession and feel that I have the drive and commitment to successfully follow a career of this type. Working as a Care Assistant, I have enhanced my knowledge of the needs of patients and their relatives in various departments. My duties include personal care of the patient, bathing, dressing, feeding and laundry. While at work, I am responsible for informing and reporting any sudden changes in the condition of the patient as well as maintaining confidentiality and attending training sessions to upgrade my knowledge, so as to meet the standards and expectations of the quality of patient care. These duties have given me more experience, helped me to cope with difficult situations by using my initiative, and helped me to be more sympathetic and more concerned about the wellbeing and feelings of others. In spite of my duties, I am able to keep my work and family commitments in balance.

In my spare time, I enjoy reading current affairs, folktales with my children and cooking multicultural dishes. I am confident that I will be a dedicated and diligent student, and studying at your institute of excellence will equip and prepare me for a successful career in Osteopathy.

PGCE

Example 73

I have always had a longstanding ambition to become a primary school teacher in order to create a beneficial learning environment for others. My own experience of education at all levels has been very positive, giving me the confidence to explore my academic potential. Assisting at a junior school has confirmed my enjoyment of and flair for working with this age group, and after starting my own family I am now in a position to commit myself fully to a PGCE.

Completing a degree in Psychology has given me experience of many areas directly relevant to teaching young children, such as studying the intellectual development of young minds, and how involving all of the senses in the learning process can aid memory retention. Modules focusing on social development and behavioural psychology have helped me to understand the range of factors involved in creating an environment conducive to learning, including ensuring pupils feel secure, respected and able to express themselves. I feel that having a scientific understanding of children's behaviour will also help me in developing good classroom management. In my PGCE I am particularly excited about acquiring increased responsibility in the classroom, and learning from current practitioners about different teaching methodologies. I also look forward to enhancing my knowledge of the National Curriculum and to the opportunity to discuss educational issues with others, as I believe there is always something to be gained from listening to others' experiences and opinions.

Assisting at a local junior school has involved supporting the teacher in her general classroom duties, giving me a realistic appreciation of a teacher's working day, helping reading groups with their literacy and helping to organise the nativity play. This placement has given me confidence in my ability to have a strong presence in the classroom and to be an effective teacher. Previously I have worked part time at a primary school, assisting children aged between five and seven in all areas of the curriculum including Literacy, Maths, Art and PE. Whilst in Sixth Form I was also involved in a Literacy Buddy scheme, using my patience and interpersonal skills to build a relationship of trust with the Year 7 pupils I helped. This was my introduction to the rewarding nature of teaching and to the idea of a career making a positive contribution to young people's lives. Having my own child has increased my responsibilities, widened my perspective on life and given me first hand experience of children's needs and developmental stages. Before September I will be continuing to gain further experience in schools.

Working in the Housing Department of my local Council has developed in me further transferable skills. My position involves frequent interaction with colleagues and the public both in person and over the telephone, equipping me with effective communication skills and an appreciation of cohesive and supportive teamwork. Resolving tenant queries also requires me to use organisation, initiative and flexibility in taking responsibility for my own caseload. Frequent use of computers in my job has made me fully IT literate, which will be useful both during my PGCE and in my career. In my leisure time I enjoy playing tennis and working out at the gym, and am an active member of a cultural society. After gaining QTS I envisage myself continually enhancing my professional skills and I hope to take the Advanced Teaching Diploma and possibly a Masters. I am a dedicated, ambitious student with both the ability and commitment to forge a successful career in teaching.

Example 74

My own experiences at school, particularly the input of my Maths and Drama teachers who encouraged me to achieve my personal best, have inspired me to enter teaching myself. In Drama, my teacher's enthusiasm and commitment motivated me to put as much effort as possible into producing high grades in coursework presentations. In Maths I initially had difficulties, but benefited from a teacher who used an innovative approach to teach us mnemonics and other memory aids which made learning more accessible.

Teaching English and Drama on a Student Teaching Programme at a Summer School I was able to help children learn verbal, written and emotional expression. The Summer School is a programme that involves both classroom teaching and extra-curricular activities, such as sports and arts, aimed at ESL students aged 11 to14. As well as classroom based teaching, I involved myself in sports and art clubs and all teachers were actively involved in personal and pastoral care. In particular I found satisfaction conveying my enthusiasm for my subjects, and in doing so helped the students to develop confidence and a better understanding of English. Following a week of training prior to the Summer School, I implemented the ideas I learnt there, such as finding new ways to present familiar concepts. At the Summer School I also worked as Head of the Drama department and of the Radio Media course, and as a group leader, supervising and motivating a team of student teachers. In these roles I was required to participate in planning the overall structure of the courses, prepare my lesson plans and organise extra-curricular events and activities. A trip to Kenya to assist in an orphanage and school allowed me to utilise these skills, and I enjoyed encouraging the Kenyan children to express themselves through language, music and art. I have also worked with much younger children on international summer courses during each of my university vacations.

During my university degree I have become familiar with class discussion and group presentations, which have been useful when preparing my own written work and analysing that of others. In English I have greatly appreciated studying a wide range of texts, representing voices from different time periods and cultures, analysing period and context. Literature of any language can be used to access the perceptions and ideas concurrent with the text and can be used as an accessible introduction to many other subjects, such as History, Politics and Science. I believe that an understanding of the literature of one's own language is fundamental to a thorough appreciation of the culture and heritage of that language and I look forward to instilling such curiosity in my pupils.

Outside of study I have maintained participation in a range of extra-curricular activities such as helping to run a children's theatre company and assisting in the delivery of a Drama Club at a local FE college. These experiences have widened my perception of the teaching profession and I have learnt from all those I have worked alongside. As a highly motivated, experienced and positive student I hope to continue this learning process during my PGCE and throughout my career.

Pharmacy

Example 75

My career goal is to become a community pharmacist as it will combine my interest in the sciences with the opportunity of having day-to-day contact with a wide range of people. This appeals to me greatly as it would involve me using my communication and interpersonal skills constantly. To work as a pharmacist has been my ambition since leaving school. Unfortunately, personal difficulties after completing my A levels prevented me from studying at university straight away. Now, after several years in an unfulfilling job, I can truly appreciate the opportunity of higher education and the need for a rewarding career.

At school I most enjoyed studying Chemistry and its applications. My main interest was in practical activities such as laboratory work and I would like to continue in this area whilst making a positive contribution to the community. On my current course I am making the most of the opportunity to prepare for degree level study and I have enjoyed this return to education, particularly the chance to discuss topics of interest with other students and to refresh my study skills. During my degree I am looking forward to developing my understanding of the mechanisms and actions of different drugs and how such knowledge can be used to treat medical conditions and alleviate pain. The anatomy and physiology of the human body and its systems fascinates me and I am looking forward to learning how pathology can be used to help cure illnesses or alleviate symptoms. I also look forward to the opportunity to practise clinical skills on placement and to study the wider role of pharmacy in the community, such as the importance of counselling and communication skills and of understanding professional law and ethics.

To confirm my interest in this career, I have an ongoing shadowing placement at my local Boots pharmacy. From observing the pharmacist, I have learnt that excellent communication skills and sensitivity are vital, as is patient confidentiality, as many customers may be in pain or confused. After discussing and observing the career with professionals in this field, I feel that this career will offer me a great deal of personal satisfaction. I look forward to active involvement with patients and I believe it is important that the pharmacist is fully accessible to the community. Having thoroughly enjoyed returning to learning I am approaching this career change as one which will require a constant effort to keep up to date with scientific developments.

My employment history has equipped me with transferable skills applicable both to life as a student and my future career. As a taxi driver, I maintain a calm and confident approach to dealing with the many people I meet each day and I enjoy this interpersonal interaction. Working long shifts has taught me the skills of self-motivation and discipline and has also illustrated to me the benefits of a university education. As a mature applicant I have had the time to consider my options thoroughly and I believe I can contribute a level headed, motivated and appreciative approach to the student body. I am fully committed to my ambition of becoming a community pharmacist and I believe I have the skills and personal qualities to achieve that goal.

Example 76

My interest in Pharmacy arose after hearing my grandfather's tales of his role as a traditional healer in his village, using natural products to cure people's conditions. He also witnessed first hand the advantages that the regular hospital could offer patients such as my asthmatic grandmother. This has stimulated my fascination with the role traditional knowledge has played in the development of medicines but I am also keen to learn more about its shortcomings and about the benefits of modern pharmaceutical practices.

At school I have found the practical aspects of Chemistry, such as the reactions of elements and compounds, particularly absorbing and I would like to understand more about the mechanisms behind these experiments and their application in medical science. In Biology I have enjoyed learning about the activities of enzymes, antibodies and antigens and I am especially interested in their role in Pharmacy. At school I have worked hard to take full advantage of the opportunity to learn and I have won several academic prizes, such as recent ones for Biology and for overall achievement in the Sixth Form.

It is my ambition to become a pharmacist, combining my interest in the subject with my desire to have a challenging career at the heart of the community. Work experience shadowing a pharmacist gave me a useful insight into the realities of daily life in this field. I found the busy environment and the high degree of face-to-face work with the public appealing. Whilst working at the pharmacy I was given responsibility for stock-taking and re-ordering, which has familiarised me with the most frequently used treatments. As a competitive student who enjoys mental challenges, I also appreciate the need to take a 'lifelong learning' approach to the career, constantly updating the necessary skills and knowledge.

Working for the Accident Volunteers of Tanzania charity, in my home country, has increased my understanding of working in a pressurised and sometimes stressful medical environment. My main duties were as a volunteer accident traffic warden, using my initiative and self-reliance to control traffic in the case of an accident. I have undergone training in lifting accident victims safely and in methods of rescuing people from a compressed car, as well as advanced First Aid that has introduced me to basic medical knowledge.

On becoming Deputy Head Boy at college I have played an important role in the school community, working on my leadership skills and self-confidence. My tasks included supporting and motivating our house team in the Inter-House Quiz, in which we took first place. I also served on a team of regular prefects for three years during which emphasis was placed on setting a good example to younger pupils. At my church I hold the position of Youth Counsellor, in which I help to motivate the children and take responsibility for our budgeting, record keeping and cash handling. This has given me experience of working with people from all backgrounds and ages, helping me to develop a mature and diplomatic approach.

Being captain of the school team, football is important to me both as a sociable outlet for stress and in helping to maintain my physical health. I have also won several awards in track and field and I intend to make full use of the sports facilities available at university. As a self-motivated and dedicated student I feel I have the qualities needed to fulfil my goal of becoming a community pharmacist, combining my interest in this area of science with the desire to work with the public to touch people's lives positively.

Philosophy

Example 77

On starting my AS Philosophy last year I had little understanding of the nature of the subject but was intrigued by the prospect of studying famous names such as Aristotle and Socrates. Through the course of my studies I discovered with fascination that Philosophy is a part of every other academic subject as well as underlying all aspects of human thought and behaviour. Moral philosophy has captivated me in particular with the opportunity to ask such questions as how and why people function as social, political, moral and creative beings. My RS A level has complemented this and I have been able to contribute to discussions on birth control, euthanasia, human rights and the nature of religion from a range of perspectives. I was also excited to find that even the study of subjects such as Biology can be enhanced using Philosophy, in areas such as the nature of consciousness and how this relates to the physiology of the brain.

To supplement my A levels I enjoy wider reading and following current debates in journals such as Philosophy Today. At university I am hoping to take advantage of the Scottish system by studying a range of Humanities subjects before specialising in Philosophy, which will add considerably to my knowledge and my range of research and study skills. At school I have also enjoyed studying IT to AS level and I intend to utilise my experience in this area in creating presentations and posters. The development of Artificial Intelligence is of great interest to me, calling the 'I think, therefore I am' definition of humanity into question and casting doubt on the nature of consciousness and free will. I am looking forward to discussing these issues with experts and those who share my passion for the subject, as well as enhancing my knowledge of Historical Philosophy and the development of the main schools of thought.

As a Student Peer Counsellor I have the responsibility of supporting pupils who are having emotional difficulties.

Sometimes these problems stem from academic worries and I have enjoyed coaching younger pupils in Biology. Bullying has also been a significant issue and I have participated in several workshops with the aim of combating this problem, focusing on preventing the onset of bullying instead of just dealing with it after it has occurred. This position has been emotionally testing as the victims of bullying are usually very distressed, but it has been a major influence on my personal development and I would like to be involved in, or set up, similar projects at university.

In my free time I like to attend live music gigs, especially of new Blues bands, as I find inspiration there for my own band which I co-founded three years ago. We practise together several times a week, and have recently started doing paid performances at small local venues. Our next goal is to produce a demo track, and to save up funds for this I have been working part time at a restaurant. As a member of the waitressing team I have developed my interpersonal skills dealing with customers, managers and the chef, and am used to working in a pressurised environment.

In studying Philosophy I hope to improve my analytical skills and build a strong base of knowledge in the area before progressing to postgraduate studies in order to explore this subject further. I look forward to being a committed member of the university community and I feel I have the qualities to make a positive contribution to this field.

Example 78

Philosophy interests me as in every work I have read by the great historical philosophers I have seen that their arguments and ideas are as relevant today as they have ever been, questioning as they do the very nature of what it is to be human, to be alive and to think. It is humbling to think that people considering this issue several thousand years ago addressed it using techniques which are still usefully applied today. Having had no opportunity to go to university after leaving school, due to financial constraints, I am now in a position to focus on my personal growth and pursue my passion for Philosophy.

In order to prepare myself for tertiary level study I am studying an Access to Humanities course at college part time. This return to education has been very enjoyable, particularly being surrounded by others with whom I can discuss academic issues. I enjoy mixing with young people and I feel that mature students and school leavers can learn a lot from each other. I look forward to contributing to the student community at university. For many years I have read books and journals about Philosophy, and I have been able to observe the change in fashions of philosophical questions. For several years medical ethics were considered a major issue, particularly focusing on the rights and wrongs of birth control and euthanasia. More recently the function and appropriate status of religion has been the dominant issue. The correlation between this and contemporary global politics is obvious and I look forward to exploring this theme with reference to the great historical schools of thought. At college I have enjoyed the multidisciplinary nature of my studies and I will be approaching Philosophy with the same attitude.

My employment experience has given me a range of skills and qualities transferable to full time education. As a retail manager I have responsibility for keeping written records, ordering and monitoring stock, and supervising my team of four staff. This has given me excellent written communication and organisational skills and, having raised my family simultaneously, I am adept at managing my time and prioritising workloads. As my team includes teenage staff as well as people older than me, I am familiar with communicating and supervising others of all ages and I feel that I can get on well with anyone. At work I have had several voluntary responsibilities such as Health and Safety Officer and the Social Secretary of the company's football club. I have enjoyed these opportunities to be part of the community and intend to continue this at university.

In my free time I enjoy spending time with my grown up children, reading about current affairs and sight seeing in the local area. My family are fully supportive of my decision to go to university and feel that this an appropriate time for me to concentrate on myself after years of working and bringing up my family. To study Philosophy will be to indulge my longstanding passion for the subject and my love of education and learning for its own sake. Undertaking this degree is a personal challenge for me and one that I am determined to succeed in.

Photography

Example 79

Studying Photography at degree level will equip me with the technical and professional skills required for a future as a commercial photographer. Taking Fashion and Design courses at college has given me a wide breadth of knowledge in contemporary art, fashion and style media. I have enjoyed exploring my own creative ideas during my coursework, which consisted of organising a catwalk fashion show and providing a supporting photographic and written report. Studying IT has introduced me to software packages such as Photoshop and CorelDraw, which will be useful given the importance of image manipulation in both art and fashion photography. At university I am hoping to develop advanced camera skills, although I look forward to discovering a wide range of styles and uses of photography. My intention is to focus on fashion photography, as this is the area I wish to work in. The opportunity for broader media and cultural debate is also appealing to me, as I believe the associated transferable skills and knowledge will be valuable for a future career in the image market.

Involvement in a locally-run Photography Club, supplemented by several day workshops in different skills such as night and action photography, has taught me the basics of photography and digital imagery and provided me with the opportunity to follow wherever my diverse interests have led me. Participation in competitions at all levels has always been encouraged and, at the age of 12, I reached the national finals in the under 18 category. After several commendations and runner up certificates I recently won the national Junior Fashion Photographer of the Year prize, submitting elements of my college coursework. My industry experience has been broadened by a two-week work placement at a local newspaper office. Here I mostly shadowed the picture editor who gave me an insight into the process of commissioning photographs as well as buying from freelances and image banks, editing the images and preparing them for print. I also worked for two days in the ICT studio, where I was given the responsibility of producing the visual weather forecast, which I was very proud to see in print the next day. At university I hope to further learn how to create, manipulate and rework imagery for fashion magazines as well as the research skills to analyse contemporary photographic styles and the historical context of the development of 20th century fashion.

As a Senior Prefect, I assist the staff with the running of my school and supervise a small group of prefect helpers, which has developed my interpersonal and leadership skills. For the last two years I have helped to run a very successful Beginners Photography Club, designed to encourage students from any year to get involved. This has allowed me to influence others with my enthusiasm for photography and to make a contribution to the school community. As a Reading Mentor I have also been involved in the school literacy campaign, reading in a pair with a Year 7 ESL student. These activities have refined my communication, teamwork and organisational skills and in each of the last two years I have received the Prize for Outstanding Contribution to the School. In my free time I also enjoy playing on the school hockey and netball teams and would like to continue these sports at university.

My ambition for the future is to work as a successful freelance fashion photographer, having my work published in magazines such as Vogue and Arena, and I believe that I have the motivation, technical skill and artistic flair to make this possible.

Example 80

Since its invention in the 19th century, photography has been the media of choice to document and record transient and non-permanent aspects of society from family life to forensic evidence. Taking my own photographs, and observing people's varying reactions to being photographed, has motivated me to reflect on the function of the photograph as a research tool. A degree in Photographic Studies will allow me to discuss and develop my views on these and other topics whilst developing my practical photography skills to an advanced level.

At school, A level Photography introduced me to formal study of the subject and I have enjoyed learning to develop and print film, to bring an imaginative approach to the medium and to analyse and evaluate my own and other artists' work. Art A level has widened my creative scope and allowed me to combine photography with other media in my work. The history of Art element has set my studies in the context of various developing artistic movements and stimulated my interest in how the dominant artistic movement of the time affects the interpretations of a viewer. My development as a photographer has also been helped by my IT studies and my hobby of designing graphics for new web sites, using my own digital images and scanned photographs. This has familiarised me with software packages such as Photoshop, Pagemaker, Illustrator, Flash and Dreamweaver and which application each is most suited to. At university I am looking forward to building on my A levels in all areas of conventional and digital photography, and in more specialist subjects such as mural printing, visual articulation and the critical debate of theoretical topics.

Aside from schoolwork I am heavily involved in music. I play the clarinet in the school Jazz Band and Orchestra and have rehearsed and performed with the National Youth Theatre for several years. The commitment of time and energy associated with this has taught me dedication, self-discipline and motivation and I have experienced the rewards of these through my love of performing. In the

Sixth Form I was awarded the Leadership Award for my role in organising and supervising the end of year ball, which also utilised time management skills and the ability to prioritise whilst multi-tasking. Taking part in the Duke of Edinburgh Award has been a very enjoyable way to meet new people and learn new skills. Since beginning the Bronze Award I have learned Spanish from scratch, and am now able to hold a conversation in a wide range of situations, as well as volunteering as a shop assistant for Oxfam. The expeditions have taught me the value of good communication in achieving effective teamwork, and have enabled me to visit new areas of the country. Having completed Silver last year I am now working towards Gold and will continue to do so at university.

After my degree I intend to progress to postgraduate studies, perhaps in Visual Culture or the History of Photography. In the future I envisage myself in a research or theoretician role, and I intend to make the most of the opportunities available at university in order to achieve this.

Physics

Example 81

The potential interrelations of Physics and Computer Technology are vast, and it has been through studying A level courses in both that I began to notice exactly how inter-linked they are. The unique creative possibilities that a greater knowledge and understanding of Physics and Computer Technology will bring are essential within my chosen field of work: aeronautical design and craft study. Studying these subjects to degree level will develop both my practical and analytical skills, and help me to understand in greater depth the processes and systems needed for the computerised manipulation of the aircraft designed. Both Physics and Computer Technology are subjects that are incredibly relevant and essential to our society and studying them will undoubtedly allow me to succeed in many different fields of employment.

I have pursued two work experience placements, which have confirmed my interest in Physics and Computer Technology. They showed me, albeit in a limited way, the interface between pure science and computer systems. I have spent a period of work experience at an aeronautical engineering firm responsible for manufacturing light aircraft and gliders. I was able to see the designs manipulated and tested on the screen before they were built, eliminating the potential of wasting millions of pounds on building designs that were likely to fail. This period of work experience improved my computer literacy as well as developing other skills, such as responsibility, teamwork, communication, listening skills and working to deadlines. Using computers in direct relation to Physics and Engineering confirmed the possible unity of my two favourite areas of study.

I am so committed to succeed within a computing environment that I have completed a CLAIT course in my spare time, as well as helping build a web site. As part of my Design and Technology course I have been developing my CAD skills extensively by producing a range of 3D models in Pro-Desktop. I was also rewarded with an 'outstanding effort' certificate in Design and Technology, further outlining my passion and dedication for the subject. This has also contributed to my desire to enter the field of aeronautical engineering through a possible postgraduate course at university when I have completed my undergraduate degree.

Out of school, I have a wide variety of interests. Since the age of eight I have been ice-skating locally, and now compete in small competitions around the country. My love of the winter sports have been furthered by a two-week skiing course, a largely unsuccessful yet highly enjoyable month spent snowboarding in France, and just recently this year, playing ice-hockey for the local team. Within school I have been Captain of the Netball and Hockey teams. My involvement in sport has developed my leadership and teamwork skills as well as showing me the dedication that is required to learn and develop. I also enjoy music concerts and have taken up the bass guitar, which I am teaching myself. I have also completed numerous courses in swimming, sailing, windsurfing, and snorkelling. I have travelled extensively around the world visiting Asia, the Middle East, America, South America, and Europe.

I believe the courses I am studying, combined with the knowledge and skills I have gained out of school in work experience and sporting pursuits will be particularly useful for the challenge of degree level study at university. I am dedicated to a successful degree in Physics and Computer Technology, followed by an even more successful career in the field.

Example 82

Physics is very challenging by nature and it is particularly satisfying to address its more demanding aspects. Problem-solving especially appeals to me, as does the requirement for intellectual commitment when addressing this subject at a higher level. It is because of these reasons that I believe Physics is the perfect degree course for me.

My interest in the subject was first ignited in my first year of secondary school. I was fascinated by the study of forces and particularly enjoyed seeing the mechanics of physical principles in such minute detail. The ability to measure and to see such fundamental components of nature in action amazed me, and sparked my desire to better understand the mechanics of the world in which I live. Studying Physics at A level allowed me to continue this fascination further and confirmed to me that it is the subject I wish to continue with at degree level.

My other A level subjects perfectly complement my studies in Physics; Mathematics allows me to better understand the basic principles of Physics, employing the same logical process and providing me with a deeper understanding of the numerical knowledge within equations and formulae; Economics allows me to apply that same understanding in a practical context and develop my numerical skills even further.

Earlier this year I gained international work experience, spending two weeks as an English teaching assistant in one of the largest colleges in Budapest. My time there was invaluable; it provided me with the opportunity to experience a completely different environment, and enabled me to develop my public speaking and people skills.

I am very involved with charity work, having spent the past two summers working for The Red Cross. As part of this scheme, I have visited Romania and Morocco after raising £2,500 for projects such as school building and well excavation, through a variety of fundraising events and jobs. I also spent four weeks travelling in Thailand with a group from school. It was one of the most rewarding experiences of my life, particularly our time spent working in an orphanage on the Thai-Burmese border. During this time I also undertook the role of accountant, and was responsible for monitoring and analysing the finances for our group of sixteen people. It was an interesting challenge tackling the variety of problems which arose whilst living on such a tight budget.

During my period of fundraising I also had a very enjoyable and rewarding time working as a crèche-volunteer, where I had responsibility for a small group of 12–20-month-old children every Saturday morning.

I am an enthusiastic artist, continuing with my Art A level, and enjoy visiting the numerous galleries around London and creating my own pieces, both in school and in my spare time. I also enjoy the violin and the drums, both of which I play to Grade 6, and singing, in which I have a distinction at Grade 4, and participate in the school gospel choir. I was able to combine my love of performing with my love of singing when taking both major and supporting roles in several middle school productions.

I am confident that my commitment to my subject and to continuing my academic career at your institution make me an ideal candidate to study Physics, and I eagerly await the challenges and opportunities that Higher Education will bring.

Physiotherapy

Example 83

Having experienced physiotherapy first hand, both on a personal and a more distant level, I have been inspired by the opportunities the profession offers to combine my interpersonal skills with my interest in the human anatomy and physiological aspects of health and wellbeing. My first experience of physiotherapy was when accompanying a close relative through his recovery and rehabilitation from a double leg amputation. This direct experience demonstrated the central aim of improving people's health and wellbeing, as well as the hands on approach. The diversity of the profession also attracts me as I feel it offers tremendous opportunities for professional development and personal satisfaction.

Since leaving school I have spent time developing many of the core interpersonal and professional skills that are essential to work in a caring environment with vulnerable people. After school I began working as a lifeguard, developing my communication and interpersonal skills through working with people of all ages. This also required me to attend training such as First Aid, and to use these skills in emergencies as required. In order to ensure my professional development, I began a two-year diploma in Sports Injuries Therapy, which gave me an insight into the basic principles of anatomy and physiology, client interaction and problem-based learning. I developed my communication, teamwork and caring skills through presenting projects to groups, communication classes and practical classes with my peers. The course also helped me to gain independence, initiative and maturity in order to direct my learning and meet assignment deadlines. At university I am looking forward to utilising the study skills I have acquired to date, broadening my knowledge of anatomy and physiology, and studying areas of particular interest such as respiratory and coronary care, and care of the elderly.

In order to investigate my chosen career more thoroughly, I undertook voluntary work experience at a physiotherapy clinic. My duties assisting and shadowing a chartered physiotherapist involved working on reception and greeting clients and gave me the opportunity to observe various injuries and treatments ranging from acute cervical disc injury to arthritis. The experience gave a context to my studying of physiotherapy and sports injuries and gave me the chance to utilise my personal qualities, strengthening my passion and enthusiasm for pursuing such a rewarding career. At present I work full-time as a bank assistant. This involves delivering a high level of customer service and using my initiative to deal with any problems as they arise. I feel it has helped me develop my interpersonal and organisational skills when dealing with customers, along with my assertiveness and confidence when making important decisions. In the evenings I enjoy part-time study in Beauty Therapy. Although I do not wish to work within the beauty industry long term, this provides me with experience of client interaction and allows me to refresh my anatomy and physiology knowledge.

In my leisure time I enjoy attending the gym and swimming twice a week, to allow me time to relax and exercise. I also take part in Pilates classes one evening per week to de-stress and re-energise. Furthering my study in the UK will allow me to make use of exceptional academic facilities and opportunities for career development. My intention is to practice within the NHS, gaining wide experience over several years, before perhaps working either abroad or in private practice. As a mature student I feel I have used my time productively since leaving school and I look forward with great excitement to the challenges and rewards of university life and study.

Example 84

After several years as a Fitness Instructor I am now working for the NHS as a Physiotherapy Technician and would like to train in Physiotherapy in order to develop my knowledge and technical skills, and to widen my scope as a healthcare professional.

In my present job as a Physio Tech I have learnt a great deal about working in a hospital environment, and the range of career paths available in this field. With extensive experience of Trauma and Orthopaedics, I have also worked in Care of the Elderly, Community, Stroke and Out-Patients. I have been inspired by the multi-disciplinary team I am part of and have thoroughly enjoyed the responsibilities of working at the acute end of this field. As well as instructing and encouraging my patients in their rehabilitation towards full health and independence, I have the responsibility of organising out-patient referrals and assessing a patient's suitability for discharge. At the weekly Multi-Disciplinary Team Meeting I contribute to discussions about patients' present conditions and future plans.

Working closely with a range of medical and care professionals I have developed confident interpersonal skills with people of all ages, levels and backgrounds, and have seen first hand the need for strong communication in ensuring cohesive teamwork. I am also responsible for our Early Health Assessment groups, which allow patients to remain fully informed about the procedures they will undergo and gives them the opportunity to ask any questions they may have. Making difficult decisions regarding patient discharge, and working in trauma, has familiarised me with the stresses associated with the pressurised environment of a hospital but ultimately I have found this to be more than compensated by the rewards of helping people to improve their future quality of life.

My previous experience as a Gym and Fitness Instructor has provided useful knowledge for dealing with sports injuries, and I feel both this and my Physio background will give me a useful context for my degree studies. At university

I am looking forward to studying the musculoskeletal network and pathologies of the spine, and to increasing my understanding of the function and movements of muscles. As a Fitness Instructor I developed an interest in and understanding of healthy and problematic movement of the body, which I hope to build on. Women's health and neuroscience are further areas of interest, and I will particularly enjoy utilising my practical and interpersonal skills during placements. My employment history has also ensured I have excellent organisational, record keeping and time management skills which will be usefully transferred to both my degree and my future career.

Outside work I enjoy practising yoga and pilates, which are excellent ways to relax and maintain health, as well as cycling and hiking with my dog. I also enjoy travelling and have worked abroad, and found this helped me develop confidence and flexibility. It has also helped me to appreciate different cultures and languages and I intend to involve myself in encouraging a higher diversity of ethnic minorities into the allied health professions. In the future I hope to advance my expertise in Orthopaedics and to work with joint replacement patients in a community setting. As a mature applicant with extensive experience in Physiotherapy, I have been able to research my options thoroughly and I feel I will be entering this profession with a realistic understanding of both its rewards and its challenges. I am very excited about the prospect of returning to education and intend to make the most of this opportunity to develop my professional potential as a Physiotherapist.

Politics

Example 85

The development of governments, their policy making and their ideological oppositions has been the most influential factor on the shaping of human society as we know it. Studying Politics will allow me to pursue this interest in how and why the world functions as it does. As Philosophy has formed the basis of almost all academic thought, from physics to religion, I feel it will enhance the depth of my knowledge and equip me with skills of enquiry which can be transferred to any area of study.

My A levels have introduced me to topics such as the French and Russian revolutions which demonstrate effectively the crossover between the disciplines of modern political history and philosophy. An awareness of the impact of Stalinism on the Soviet Union, for example, is extremely useful when analysing and evaluating the theoretical qualities of communist ideology. At university I am looking forward to studying the development of dictatorships throughout the world, comparing the notorious figures of Western Europe with some of the lesser studied rulers of developing countries. The political ramifications of anarchist movements also interest me, as does continuing my study of communism, the enormous ramifications of which continue today. I also have an active interest in the history, causes and prevention of racism and I hope to explore this from an academic stance.

Travelling to Russia and the former East Germany I have found the contrast in culture, architecture and attitudes when compared to western Europe enlightening. Even more illuminating was the palpable difference in these factors when I returned to the area after a five-year gap, stimulating my reflection on the problems and issues associated with the fall of communism. At school I enjoy any opportunity for debate. Discussion with others allows me to learn from their experiences and to refine and develop my own views. In a 'Youth Speaks' competition I was Chairman of a team of three, and found this furthered my confidence in public speaking. My efforts in school have been rewarded by prizes and commendations for Hardworking Pupil, Schoolwork and Conduct, and I will bring the same level of commitment to my degree.

As Class Student Representative I was responsible for presenting the views of my peers to staff, and enjoyed this contribution to the school community. Supervising the rescue boat in the Sailing Club developed my abilities in this sport. My three years in the Army and Navy Cadets featured a continual emphasis on teamwork, leadership, discipline and focus. A Duke of Edinburgh expedition on Dartmoor enabled me to utilise this experience, to develop my interpersonal skills working closely with others, and to acquire new skills of map reading and camp craft. A two-day activity course contributed to this character building. In my leisure time I enjoy travelling around the country to compete in strategy game contests, as well as playing bass and electric guitar and taking part in volleyball, rowing and hockey clubs.

In the future I intend to go into teaching and this broad based degree will provide a sound background for educating others in the Humanities, as well as giving me useful experience of critical analysis and argument, and of solving theoretical and practical problems. I am a hardworking and highly motivated student and I look forward to meeting the challenges of university life.

Example 86

Politics has always played a significant part in my life; my father is a local Councillor, and, when we lived in America, my mother ran for Governor of our State. Indeed, coming from a transatlantic background, I was particularly interested in the element of my A level Politics course that concerned the comparative study of the British and American systems of government. I found it fascinating to analyse the two states from a historical perspective, to examine their different origins and to assess how those origins have influenced the nature of their political structures today. During my time in the Sixth Form, I thoroughly enjoyed the study of Politics, Economics and History, but I found my Politics course to be especially rewarding and would relish the opportunity to continue it at university.

Studying Politics at A level has given me a unique opportunity to become more socially aware of the issues affecting both Britain and the United States, and has allowed me to become more informed and selective as a voter. In particular, the development of American racial tensions and the relative effectiveness of American and British elections have proved two topics that carry a great deal of weight within my own life, meaning that I have put great effort into doing well in my studies and have often undertaken further reading in my spare time. Indeed, I have developed an interest in the role of the United States on the global stage, particularly its relationship with Europe, and I have pursued this by reading such articles as Robert Kagan's 'Power and Weakness', Samuel Huntington's 'The Clash of Civilisations', and Francis Fukuyama's 'The End of History'.

I found Fukuyama's perception of liberalism as the pinnacle of human political development to be especially interesting in the context of current debates over globalisation and free trade. I always try to take an analytical approach when considering new points of view, and try to use them to complement and question rather than replace opinions that I have previously held.

In addition to a strong commitment to my studies, I have always played an active role in student government as an elected member of the Sixth Form Committee and of the School Council. I also ran in our recent mock elections, which involved learning about and understanding the process of political elections from all perspectives involved. I found this particularly complemented my studies of the electoral process in A level Politics, and gaining first-hand experience of elections meant that I achieved a mark of 97% in my Electoral Process coursework. I developed my writing skills and teamwork through my contribution to the school magazine, and my powers of advocacy as a member of the Debating Society. In my spare time, I enjoy swimming, photography, astronomy, and mountain bike racing; I hope to continue these activities at university by making use of the facilities on offer.

I am certain that studying for a degree in Politics will help me to develop the analytical skills required to fulfil my career aspirations of journalism or Local Government, but ultimately my motivation for studying the subject runs much deeper than this. The study of Politics at A level has, for me, raised more questions than it has answered; by continuing the subject at university, I would hope to answer some of these questions, but also to raise many more. I take pride in taking a tenacious, independent approach to my studies and hope that this will serve me well during my time at university, and I look forward to the challenges university will bring.

Psychology

Example 87

It is human nature to question everything or try to make sense of life; I believe that through its many perspectives, Psychology has the potential to answer a great deal of these questions. Psychology is accessible because not only is it a scientific study of thought and behaviour, it is also an art that can be applied by the individual to everyday life. Psychology is a unique subject as it is all around us at all times; it is in the media, in hospitals and schools, and in every person on Earth. Studying Psychology to degree level will allow me to explore all aspects of human behaviour and the psyche in order to forge an eventual career in the field.

Although I did not choose Psychology as one of my AS subjects, I feel that my current studies have prepared me for such a course. Biology has given me a good grounding in the physical side of Psychology; a module on the human brain last term will be particularly useful during the course of my Psychology degree. Maths has improved my observational and analytical skills, strengthening my ability to interpret data and allowing me to draw logical answers. English Literature has developed my ability to think critically and it was through the exploration of character that I became even more interested in Psychology.

As Psychology is an integrated part of Philosophy, I was able to further my interests in both by attending a Philosophy club at my school. Here, I debated topical issues and learnt to articulate my views as well as considering and respecting the views of others. More importantly, Philosophy club introduced me to a broad range of extra reading materials, many of which concerned Psychology. Since choosing to undertake a Psychology degree I have made a concentrated effort to read around my subject; I have a subscription to Psychology Review and have recently met Mike Caldwell, a leading Psychologist attached to the University of Bath.

As a member of the Sixth Form Council, I am proud to have been part of a team that pioneered a new pupil mentoring scheme in Lower School, helping students with homework and any personal problems they may have. Since the scheme began, the school has reported a 27% drop in bullying and a significant rise in extra-curricular participation. Being a member of an efficient, focused team has meant that my organisational and communication skills have undoubtedly improved, and I have taken great personal satisfaction from being involved in such a committee.

I have received many academic awards and certificates for excellent performance and effort in all my school subjects. I enjoy sports and have represented my school in netball and athletic tournaments, gaining first, second and third place medals and certificates. I have also achieved my Duke of Edinburgh Bronze award and I am aiming towards my Silver level Award.

I would describe myself as a success-driven, self-disciplined and conscientious, hard working student. I have increased in confidence and self-belief through my time in Sixth Form, and can only hope that university will have an equally positive effect on me. Studying Psychology will allow me to pursue a career in the field, and a deeper understanding of the subject will be beneficial in terms of many life skills.

Example 88

Through a determined focus on extra-curricular reading using all media available to me, I have widened my knowledge and appreciation of Psychology as a subject and am convinced that I am suited to studying it at degree level. Studying Psychology at college gave me the basis for continued study throughout my spare time, leading to a new confidence in experimental data analysis as well as a broader basic knowledge of the subject. I particularly like the fact that Psychology encompasses many of the areas included in the Scottish Higher exams that I sat last year; the analytical skills of English Literature, the science of Biology and the logical thinking of Maths. Above all, I have chosen to study Psychology in order to fulfil a long-term interest in the complexity of human behaviour and psyche.

My Year 11 work experience included working in a laboratory environment for a local leather company. This was very science-based, encompassing many of the key skills needed to work in a laboratory such as immaculate hygiene, precise attention to detail and patience. This has direct relevance to working in the field of Psychology; I hope to enter Clinical Psychology and so will potentially spend a large proportion of time within a laboratory environment.

Currently, I am involved in assisting teachers at a School for the Disabled. I am in a class with young autistic children and I find the work very enjoyable. I have gained a lot of experience in how autism affects behaviour and personality, and have made many new young friends. Seeing the effect that a brain disorder can have on both the people suffering from it and their immediate family is quite moving; my Higher in Biology also gives me a good grounding when it comes to a Psychology degree in learning more about autism and why it occurs.

The main pull of Psychology, for me, is how relevant it is to our everyday existence. I think one interesting application of Psychology in life is advertising and the media. I find that the Psychology behind some adverts can be very intriguing, and shows that the topic is very significant in today's media. I believe that Psychology is an indispensable subject, in that there is a wealth of information still to be uncovered; information that can teach us about ourselves, about others and about the social world in which we live.

I have lived in and visited several different countries throughout my life, including New Zealand and Indonesia. This experience has resulted in a growing curiosity in other cultures. I believe that this has broadened my horizons and is likely to make me a more rounded and valuable future employee. Additionally, I find it increasingly interesting to examine the psychology behind culture, especially in light of recent problems concerning religious-based terror attacks; does culture shape our psyche, or does our collective psyche shape culture?

I have no doubt that university will be a challenging yet fulfilling part of my life, and hopefully will be the beginning of a successful career. I intend to dedicate myself fully to further study and cannot wait for the opportunities that are ahead.

Radiography

Example 89

My fascination with the subject of Radiography stems from my love of technology, and my interest in anatomy and physiology. I greatly enjoyed my A level choices of Biology, Chemistry and Psychology, which I chose for a number of reasons. Firstly, I thought they would be useful for my chosen career in Radiography: Biology and Chemistry because of the scientific nature of the job, and Psychology because I thought it would be useful to help me understand how people think and behave. Secondly, I was good at sciences and enjoyed doing them.

During my time in the Sixth Form I took a number of steps to prepare myself for studying Radiography. As well as reading up on the subject, I undertook work experience at a large teaching hospital in the Radiography department. Here I gained insights into the routine work of Radiographers through taking part in ward rounds and viewing, first-hand, how their work impacts on the patients. In this sense, I have come to appreciate the people-centred approach to health care, which has added a new and exciting dimension to my interest in the science. As part of this shadowing I attended a Radiography open day where I got the opportunity to talk to experts in the field about the wide and varied range of duties performed by Radiographers. The scope of the job, from dealing with paediatric and geriatric cases to the post-operative treatment of patients, I found to be an immensely exciting prospect. These experiences have served to affirm my conviction that Radiography represents the ideal career for me.

I have gained valuable work experience by recently taking up a part-time job as a shop assistant. My duties and responsibilities include stock taking, cashing up at the end of the day, serving customers and dressing the shop floor. This experience has given me a number of transferable skills, including the ability to work within a team, confidence when communicating with a range of people, and the ability to organise myself and manage my time more effectively.

In terms of the course, I am most interested in Therapeutic Radiography, although I am equally keen to learn about the Diagnostic side. Modules I am particularly looking forward to studying include 'Behavioural Sciences', 'Radiation Science and Technology' and 'Clinical Practice'. I am most excited about the opportunity the course will give me to apply my knowledge of anatomy and physiology to patient conditions, as well as learn about the different types of cancers in different parts of the body and how they can be treated using radiotherapy.

I take pride in leading an active life outside of school. I have played in a local football team for the past two seasons, and regularly attend a badminton club where I play competitively and also teach young children. I express my love of music through playing bass guitar in a band, with whom I have gigged both locally and nationally, most notably at an outdoor festival in Manchester. I believe that I am prepared for the hard work involved in completing a Radiography degree, and I am looking forward to marrying my fascination for the science with my conviction to play an active role in the treatment and rehabilitation of patients.

Example 90

After finding my work as a Systems Analyst insufficiently fulfilling I now wish to pursue a career as a Radiographer, providing specialist care to patients within a clinical environment. Applying a combination of scientific and technical expertise in a role which provides the flexibility to develop according to my talents appeals to me greatly and I feel I am now in a position to commit myself fully to this career change.

My previous experience of a science-based degree has ensured I am competent in the appropriate study and research skills such as self-directed learning, problem solving and the use of analytical equipment. Throughout university I was complimented on the amount of effort I invested in the course and I have always enjoyed tackling new ideas and techniques. Group research projects usually required one person to seize the initiative and organise a work schedule, and I enjoyed frequently taking on this role. In studying Diagnostic Radiography I am looking forward to amassing and assimilating the necessary information and to learning about radiographic techniques, diagnostic imaging, and the associated pathology.

As my sister works in a hospital Radiology department I have been able to learn from her and her colleagues about the types of work undertaken by Radiographers and the training involved. Listening to her enthusiastic descriptions of her work I have been excited about the prospect of a job involving a high degree of specialist knowledge about the science of radiation and the use of advanced imaging technology, alongside a high level of patient interaction. I have also been interested to learn about the range of careers available within the field, and the scope for continued development and career progression. In order to prepare fully for this career change I have organised a series of site visits to clinical departments shadowing a superintendent Radiographer. This will give me the opportunity to see first-hand what the job entails and to learn from the professionals in the area I wish to work in.

In my current role as a Systems Analyst I provide IT support for clients, using problem solving and diagnostic skills constantly and enjoying a great deal of customer contact. This has equipped me with confident interpersonal skills which will be made use of when dealing with patients, families and healthcare professionals. I am also familiar with the use of IT as an integral part of my working life and the need to frequently update my knowledge in order to achieve this successfully. Long shifts and strict deadlines have taught me how to maintain a professional and efficient approach when working under pressure. In my previous work as a Sales Assistant I dealt with customers every day and was frequently trusted to deputise for my manager in his absence.

During leisure time I enjoy playing a wide variety of sports and have been involved in several cricket and football teams during school and college. I also enjoy keeping up-to-date with the latest developments in the fields of science and IT through reading newspapers and journals. As a mature applicant with contacts in Radiology and a background in science I feel I am committing to this change of career with a realistic appreciation of both the rewards and challenges of studying and working in Radiology. I am a highly motivated individual, dedicated to making the most of this opportunity to become a healthcare specialist, and I feel I have the qualities required to succeed both at university and in my future career.

Social Work

Example 91

After finding my work in a variety of childcare and Early Years environments to be stimulating and rewarding, I am hoping to qualify as a children's social worker. As well as working towards the appropriate professional qualification, I am looking forward to studying the many different subjects, such as law, which have an impact on social work and in putting into practice my personal values of respect and equality for all.

It is my long-term ambition to pursue a career as a qualified social worker, working in the community. I particularly enjoyed the placements I undertook as part of my BTEC National Diploma in Early Years, and I am therefore strongly considering specialising in supporting children and families. The adult services area, and especially the needs of disabled adults in the community, is also of interest to me. As a social worker I would welcome the opportunity to help people through difficult times in their lives, and to promote children's interests.

During my BTEC I worked with children between the ages of 0 and 8 years, from a wide diversity of backgrounds and ethnicities. This was a great opportunity to put into practice the principles of equality and respect for diversity which we had studied in college. The placements were in a private nursery and an Early Years Centre, and I took full advantage of the opportunity to learn from the range of childcare and education practitioners I worked alongside. Learning about the differences between people, and the huge diversity of cultures and languages in Britain, is very important to me and I hope to continue to supplement this throughout my working life.

I have worked in the Reception class at a primary school, where I was able to help the children through this important first stage of their school life. I assisted in literacy and numeracy and made numerous displays of the pupils' work. The most rewarding aspect for me was in helping to empower the children, and encouraging their ability to express their interests and opinions. I have also volunteered as an assistant at a local church crèche in order to increase my experience. Being employed in a variety of childcare settings I have worked to develop a flexible approach, adapting to each situation accordingly.

In my present job as a sales adviser for Halifax Home Insurance, I deal with face to face and written enquiries from the public on a daily basis. As well as developing excellent active listening and communication skills, this position has required me to build on my natural empathy and patience when dealing with difficult customers. Working with computers everyday, I am highly competent in a range of software and in using computers to maintain high standards of organisation and efficiency. As I frequently deal with clients' issues on my own, I am accustomed to being self-motivated and using my initiative to solve problems.

Outside of work I have an active interest in the local arts scene. I often visit a local dance school in order to watch performances of contemporary dance, and I enjoy socialising at live music events. I am a positive and hardworking person, fully committed to social work as a career, and I feel I have the resilience and motivation required to succeed in this challenging and rewarding field.

Example 92

My interest in acquiring formal degree qualifications in Social Work is based on five years relevant work experience and the encouragement of my mentor in my current employment. At university I am particularly excited to expand my knowledge of Communication and Empowerment, the Management of Risk and, of course, the practical element of the course. On qualifying I would like to work for children's services and my long-term career goal is to enter management. In the short-term, I would like to work abroad and gain experience of social work in other cultures.

After leaving school I completed an award in Child Care and Education which included a year of practical experience followed by an HND in Health and Social Care. The course themes will be a sound foundation for my university studies. My work experience extends from voluntary work to managing my parents' restaurant and extensive care work based in the community. Currently I am a Homeless Support Officer, offering clients wide ranging support from an initial risk assessment to a care and support plan. Liaising with a wide variety of agencies within the county has enhanced my teamwork, diplomacy and organisational skills. As I interact well with clients, I quickly gain their trust by building a rapport and I efficiently and effectively meet client needs. I am also able to prioritise my time and meet casework deadlines, often with competing tasks, by adopting an organised and focused approach.

Through interacting with people I have developed personal qualities of patience, tolerance and empathy. I have met with many vulnerable and troubled people and have an open-minded and non-judgmental approach to situations and individuals. I have the ability to be flexible and use my initiative and problem solving skills to deal with challenging and ever diverse situations. Last year I took an evening course in Counselling Skills and Psychology. I have a thirst for knowledge and self-improvement and completing this course, whilst enhancing my day to-day activities, has also motivated me further to apply for this degree.

I have a natural ability to assume responsibility and a great capacity for hard work. This was demonstrated during my volunteer work in a US summer camp with deprived youngsters. In my second year I was promoted as a camp teacher for the subject of youth development studies, for which I designed the curriculum. During group discussions regarding self-esteem, body image, assets, media perception and status, the class was encouraged to participate both verbally and through written tasks. During my HND I was elected course representative by my peers.

In travelling extensively I have valued meeting people from other cultures, religions and backgrounds. My interests also include

horse riding (I am a member of the British Show Jumping Association), going to the gym, swimming, reading and taking part in community and local events. I believe that having a good life balance will be essential whilst attending university and also in an emotionally charged profession such as Social Work.

At university I intend to be an active member of the student community. As a mature student I will bring a wealth of experience and will approach my studies with the same determination, enthusiasm and commitment I have applied to my working life. In successfully completing my degree I will be equipped with the qualifications and knowledge to have a personally rewarding career in Social Work.

Sociology

Example 93

An increased exposure to and awareness of society and its behavioural patterns over the course of studying Sociology A level has provoked in me a profound interest in various sociological theories and ideologies, and it is this interest that has further fuelled my fascination with human interaction and compelled me to choose Sociology as a degree subject.

Studying both Sociology and Psychology A levels has taught me a great deal about myself; not least that I can be a very argumentative and opinionated individual. However, these courses have taught me how to focus these traits to produce positive personality attributes; I am still opinionated but I can form these opinions into coherent, balanced arguments, and I am always willing and ready to listen to other points of view. As a member of the Sixth Form debating team, I was able to expand on my experience of public speaking with this in mind. One of the high points of being a member of this club was debating against other schools on both international and national current affairs, at the Welsh Assembly in Cardiff. As a confident speaker I was able to fully present a well researched argument from all angles and boldly put forward my own personal views.

For my work experience in Year 11 I went to a health centre for a week. I found this most interesting as it gave me an opportunity to talk to the various workers there and most importantly discuss their attitudes to different situations that they have to face in this sort of a working environment. What intrigued me most of all was the way that the receptionist described how certain patients could be far more intimidating than others and the way they deal with these sorts of problems; aspects of the job directly relevant to Sociology. Again, I was surprised at how prevalent Sociology is, in all walks of life and in all professions.

My extra-curricular activities have included participation in the Paired Reading Literacy Scheme over the past three years, which involved working with Year 7 pupils to improve their reading skills. The twice-weekly sessions were both fun and productive, both for my assigned reading partner and myself. I found that the task required a lot of tact and patience as well as encouragement to boost my readers' confidence. One of the more testing parts of this was having to entertain and interest a less than willing younger reader in times when they felt a little vulnerable, but I approached all tasks with persistent enthusiasm and tolerance, leading to an improved confidence on the part of the Year 7 child I was reading with.

I am very fit, having attended a gym for the past two years. As well as using the weights room, I have recently taken up badminton and hockey. I would ideally like to coach children in hockey, having played it at school as well as at the centre, as I got so much satisfaction out of the Paired Reading Scheme. It would mean a dedicated focus on achieving a coaching qualification, and this is something that I would like to undertake at university by using the sports facilities made available to me as a student.

I feel that in the future I would like to dedicate my time academically towards studying a subject that helps me better understand human behaviour and nature. As an outgoing person with good communication skills I feel I would be able to contribute to this area of study and, more importantly, to the field of sociology in my future career. I see a degree in Sociology as being both a challenge and an exciting journey.

Example 94

Forming the academic basis of policy making across the public and private sectors, studying Sociology will allow me to understand the processes governing a society's function and evaluate the causes and consequences of social change. This degree will also equip me with skills in analytical and computer-based research and an awareness of social policy, which will be useful in a range of future research careers.

Through reading textbooks such as those by Haralambos and Holborn I have been able to gain a solid grounding in the differing theories on a wide range of areas, such as the family, religion and crime. It has been useful discussing these texts in class with my peers and has sparked some thought provoking debates.

Studying design movements in DT I have been intrigued by the influence of past cultures on today's designs and what this may show us about our perceptions of those societies. In Business Studies I have been interested in the emphasis on marketing in every area of business, demonstrating the importance of understanding how and why parts of society think as they do. Human resource management was another enlightening topic and I enjoyed studying how employee motivation and effective management are achieved. I am particularly looking forward to studying the sociology of workplaces during my degree. At an 'Insight to Management' course I was appointed director of a team of six, which helped to develop my leadership and problem solving skills. We went on to receive a prize for being the most profitable company.

As a Warden and Sixth Form Rep at school I have improved my initiative, time management skills, and verbal communication, representing others' views to a committee, and completing tasks to strict deadlines. Voluntary work at a Cheshire home has aided my personal development, helping others complete tasks I previously took for granted. Working with vulnerable people, and completing a Vulnerable Adults course, has also developed my awareness of different sectors of society and their varied needs. Participation in the Duke of Edinburgh scheme has developed my organisational and planning skills, which will be useful when I start university, and taught me how to listen and learn from others' experiences in a team.

At the age of eight, I joined my local rugby club, and for two years I have played for my school team. After two successful rugby tours I was recently invited on a third, to South America. I have been selected to play for Leeds and am awaiting news as to whether I have gained a place at the Yorkshire Academy. Throughout my career I have scored hundreds of tries, as well as coaching a youth team, and will be continuing to develop my rugby throughout university. I have also captained the athletics team, winning the Leeds league trophy twice. In sprinting I have broken school records and my sports have taught me the value of persistence and dedication in developing my potential. In conclusion, I look forward to the challenges of living and studying independently and intend to bring my self-motivation and positive work ethic to all aspects of university life.

Teaching

Example 95

Throughout life, my aspiration in terms of prospective careers has been shared by both education and business. The allure of a Teaching degree to me is the prospect of some day stimulating the minds of young individuals and becoming an influential figure in their lives. In truth, I believe that a Teaching degree will allow me to explore all aspects of the educational field, and provide me with an excellent basis for a career in teaching.

In my current Advanced level subjects I consider Business Studies as my forte, and this is supported by studies in Media, Sociology and History. Business Studies allows me to apply theory to real life situations, such as the theory of price elasticity within the consumer market. My current Advanced level studies are very demanding, but are the most beneficial academic programmes that I have taken part in. I enjoy the classroom teaching in a lecture style environment, but also get personal fulfilment from carrying out independent research, and adding my views to assignments that are set. I have recently enjoyed analysing the relative success and criticisms of the National Curriculum in Sociology, which included analysing evidence from theorists such as Denis Lawton. I have also gained considerable satisfaction from studying the whole of my Business course, and on a daily basis I research different forms of media in order to obtain information regarding the business world. I consider this independent learning process as very beneficial and as a characteristic of undergraduate study that will suit me.

As well as my education I regularly involve myself in extra-curricular activities. I have taken part in the Young Enterprise scheme for which I was elected deputy Managing Director and Finance Manager. This was a very challenging activity that taught me the skills of dedication, motivation, teamwork, and time keeping in order for a business to function successfully.

In all of my educational institutions, I have been honoured with roles that carry with them a high degree of responsibility and pride. In my final year at high school, I was appointed as a peer councillor for lower school pupils, special needs assistant for children with English, Maths and ICT difficulties, and was also made year representative and prefect. These are activities that have helped develop me as a person and taught me the skills of delegation, arbitration and listening as well as the vital skills needed to work with others in order to generate results.

My other hobbies include activities such as weight training, Aikido and the Duke of Edinburgh Award in which I have obtained the Bronze level and am hoping to reach Silver in the coming year. These have helped me to develop my teamworking skills and I hope to continue with these activities during my university studies. As well as my advanced studies this year, I am also attending my local primary school for three hours per week in order to gain valuable experience within the educational field. This opportunity will allow me to experience first hand a real life teaching environment and will hopefully inspire my studies throughout my degree. My choice of university reflects my longing to attend an institution that is renowned for its academic excellence in my chosen subject area, and will allow me to fulfil my potential.

Example 96

After several years working in the commercial food industry, I have become increasingly interested in a career as a teacher, using my academic and industry experience to make a positive impact on young people's lives. Teaching Food Technology, I will be able not only to share my enthusiasm and knowledge of the subject, but also to help equip my students with useful life skills. I am looking forward to taking on the responsibility of having my own classes and students and developing my own teaching skills in the appropriate environment.

My interest in teaching has been confirmed by the time that I have spent observing and assisting at a secondary school. After spending five consecutive days observing Design and Technology classes and particularly Food Technology, I am now spending one day a month there until the end of the academic year. I have found the school to be an enjoyable and positive learning environment with great enthusiasm for Food Technology from teachers and pupils. Participating in the Young Cook of the Year competition, for example, has been excellent motivation for the students to develop their creative and technical abilities with food. Coming from an industry background I have also taken a great interest in the ways in which the school encourages the students' involvement in business.

My academic and employment experience has equipped me well for the transfer to learning the art of teaching. My HND in Food Technology has provided me with a detailed overview of this subject, which has been supplemented by my work in food quality control. In 2005 I became a shift quality controller, taking on day-to-day responsibility for monitoring quality in the preparation of vegetables. Taking responsibility for raw food and microbiological sampling has furthered my technical knowledge of Food Science, and as I also had a customer liaison role I acquired strong interpersonal and verbal communication skills. Moving companies in 2006, I worked for two years as a Food Technologist. This involved daily quality auditing of convenience foods, pies and quiches, through sampling, tasting and inspection. Setting up control procedures, supporting product development trials and analysing audit results have all ensured I have a high level of administrative and organisational ability. Through the variety of positions I have held, I have also developed problem solving and critical evaluation techniques and an enjoyment of design and product development. In my current role I work with the public everyday, which I feel will be particularly useful in my future career dealing professionally with pupils, parents, teachers and other school staff.

Juggling the demands of my career with raising a young family has ensured I am familiar with managing my time well and prioritising my responsibilities. On acceptance to the scheme my immediate priority in terms of subject knowledge would be to refine my practical understanding of the use of ICT in the Food Technology curriculum, as I realise this area will continue to grow in importance. Although my employment has given me a working knowledge of the use of computers I would benefit from additional training in IT. In the future I envisage myself taking greater responsibility for my subject area within the school. My classroom observations have confirmed that I would enjoy working in this challenging and rewarding environment and I look forward to career in which no two days are alike.

Veterinary Science

Example 97

Studying Veterinary Science is the first step in fulfilling my ambition of working as a farm vet, combining my enjoyment of the practical application of the sciences with my interest in farming and its role in rural communities and economies.

A fortnight's work placement at a veterinary surgery has given me experience of handling animals and of the demands and pressures of being a vet. My work involved practical tasks such as cleaning, bathing and grooming, preparing the consultation equipment and helping to weigh and take the temperatures of small animals. Observing a consultation in which an otherwise healthy dog was put to sleep because the owner could not afford to pay for its operation was an

eye-opening introduction to the realities of veterinary practice, and I am also interested in the role funding plays in the treatment or otherwise of farm animals. Assisting at a farm part-time for several months last year gave me a different perspective of working with animals, which focused on hard physical labour, long hours and the emotional highs and lows as the farmer dealt with the births of lambs, and unexpected diseases and injuries amongst his livestock.

Through discussing issues such as Foot and Mouth Disease and the BSE crisis with the farm workers, I became interested in the role of government policies in the development of farming. Visiting different farms to monitor welfare and treat animals, and playing an integrated role in the rural community appeals to me, and I am interested to see how advances in veterinary technology and knowledge might be used to improve the lives of both the farmer and his animals. At school I have been particularly interested in Biology and Chemistry practicals and in understanding how the systems of the body contribute to the whole. Helping the Chemistry teacher to set up a science club has given me a platform to discuss ethical issues such as animal experiments with my peers, learning from other people's views and becoming confident in explaining and justifying my own, as well as allowing us to complete experiments not covered by the syllabus. I am excited by the prospect of studying all aspects of Veterinary Science, and particularly in learning the professional skills to deal with the public on a daily basis and to provide palliative care to alleviate the suffering of animals with chronic or terminal illnesses.

Having played the trumpet for several years I now lead the brass section of the National Youth Orchestra and attend regular practices as well as performing with my school's Orchestra and Jazz Band. This commitment of time and energy has been rewarded by the opportunity to take part in concert tours around the world, widening my horizons and developing my communication skills as I frequently meet and play alongside new people from different cultures and languages. As a volunteer assistant at my school I run a literacy club for Year 7 pupils, which allows me to play a responsible role in the school community. Witnessing the pupils' advances in reading ability and self-confidence is extremely rewarding, particularly with pupils whose first language is not English.

My long term aim is to practice as a vet and specialise in the treatment of farm animals, contributing to good practice in this industry. My work experience and wider reading confirms my interest and suitability for this area and I am ready for the challenges awaiting me at university.

Example 98

My early motivation to study Veterinary Science was sparked by a series of visits to our local vet as a child, during which I was fascinated by the range of animals in the waiting room and I was inspired by the realisation that one individual had the knowledge to treat all of them. This interest has developed as I have studied the Sciences in increasing depth at school.

Biology has introduced me to the incredible number of different species and subspecies in the world, and studying food chains I have been amazed by the interrelationships between them and the role each wild animal has in the ecosystem. Although most pet animals have lost this function, my work experience has shown me the important role they can still have in people's lives as companions and as assistants. In Chemistry I have particularly enjoyed experiments such as making aspirin, in which we have learnt about the chemical reactions involved in the use of drugs to alleviate pain and combat illness. At university I hope to vastly increase this knowledge and I am fascinated to learn how the same condition is treated in animals of vastly differing size and physiology.

Last year I completed two placements of two weeks each, at a small local vets practice and at a large practice specialising in complex surgery. During the first placement I was able to shadow and assist in all areas of the surgery's work, from booking appointments and cleaning up, to bathing and exercising patients and observing procedures. Shadowing consultations involving vaccinations and check ups of new puppies I was interested to note the emphasis placed on maintaining good health, through boosters and worming tablets for example, in order to prevent future illness. At the larger veterinary practice I was able to observe more complex operations and gained an appreciation of the many different roles within the team, from nursing assistants to anaesthetists. I also volunteer part-time for Pets As Therapy, which organises visits of pets to seriously ill patients in hospital. Accompanying animals on these visits and observing the impact they can have on a *patients'* health and wellbeing has been very rewarding and has given me a different perspective on the function of pet animals within society. I have also been involved in fund-raising for this charity, as I believe its work is very important.

Outside school I enjoy rock-climbing and mountaineering and have recently returned from a three-week expedition in the Himalayas. This trip involved a huge amount of advance preparation both in terms of logistics and in my own physical training. Practising my climbing skills on such demanding terrain has been a tremendous boost to my self confidence and I find it an exhilarating and enlivening hobby. Climbing over 15,000ft passes required strong teamwork as it was important that we moved together, and that each person could trust their belay partner with their life, to ensure that every participant reached the top in good health. At my church youth club I volunteer as a Leader, organising social and fund-raising events as well as providing advice and support for younger members. This has helped to develop both my leadership and interpersonal skills, as well as time management and organisation.

In conclusion, I feel that my varied and active interests, including a strong motivation to practise as a vet, will equip me well for my degree and future career and I intend to make the most of every opportunity available to me at university.

Chapter 13

Closing thoughts

Closing thoughts

The aim of this guide is to provide you with a firm idea of what you should include in your Personal Statement for application to universities in the United Kingdom. Our hope is that, by following the principles and steps contained in this guide, you will be able to compose a well-structured, convincing and ultimately successful Personal Statement.

Remember, your Personal Statement must be unique to you and convey why an admissions tutor should offer you a place to study your chosen subject at their university.

From all at BPP Learning Media we would like to take this opportunity to wish you the very best of luck with your application. We would like to wish you every success in securing your place at university.

Good luck!!

Appendix

Useful websites

Useful websites

General
Universities and Colleges Admissions Service (UCAS)
www.ucas.com

Department for Education
www.education.gov.uk

Push
www.push.co.uk

Choosing a university
Open Days
www.opendays.com

The Good University Guide
http://extras.thetimes.co.uk/public/good-university-fuidelandon

The Sunday Times University Guide
http://extras.timesoline.co.uk/strg/universityguide.php

The Guardian University Guide
http://education.guardian.co.uk/universityguide

Choosing a course
UK Course Finder
www.ukcoursefinder.com

Prospects
www.prospects.ac.uk

Fees, student loans and finance
Student Finance England
www.direct.gov.uk/studentfinance

Student Loans Company
www.slc.co.uk

The Educational Grants Advisory Service
www.family-action.org.uk

Hot Courses
www.scholarship-search.org.uk

Government Information
www.direct.gov.uk/en/Education And Learning/University
And Higher Education/index.htm

Gap year
Year Out Group
www.yearoutgroup.org

Gap Year Directory
www.gapyeardirectory.co.uk

Real Gap
www.realgap.co.uk

i-to-i
www.i-to-i.com

Community Service Volunteers
www.csv.org.uk

Raleigh International
www.raleighinternational.org

Teaching and Projects Abroad
www.projects-abroad.co.uk

Voluntary Service Organisation
www.vso.org.uk

Worldwide Volunteering
www.wwv.org.uk

Appendix

Sandwich courses
Year in Industry
www.yini.org.uk

Overseas students
British Council
www.educationuk.org

Council for International Student Affairs
www.ukcisa.org.uk

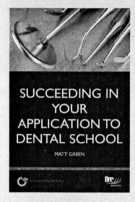